SELECTIONS FROM THE LETTERS

AND LEGAL PAPERS

of

THURMAN ARNOLD

With a Foreword by

WILLIAM O. DOUGLAS

Copyright © 1961 VICTOR H. KRAMER

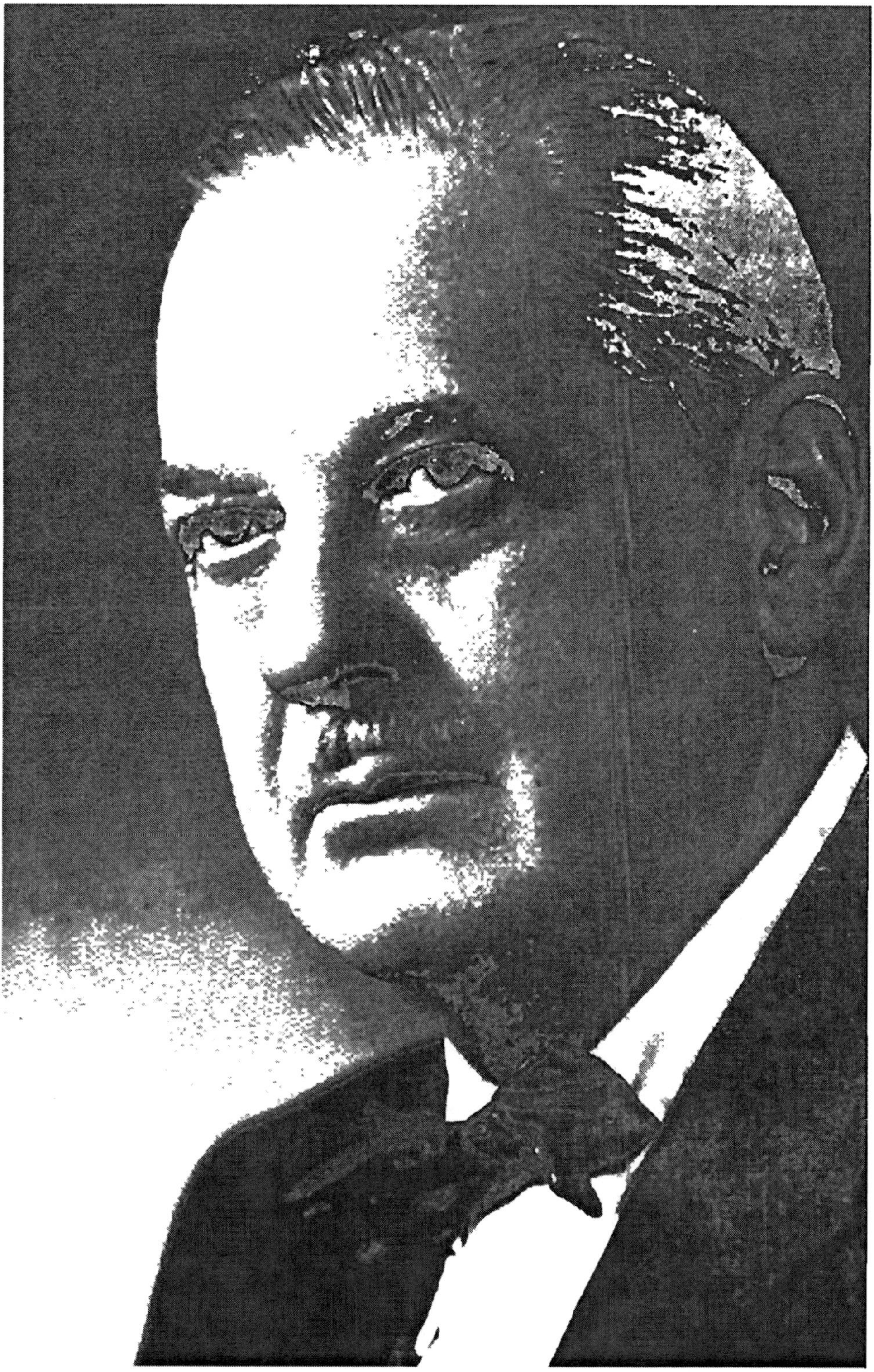

CONTENTS

Preface vi

Foreword, by William O. Douglas viii

I   Personal History 1

II   Whimsy and Pure Fun and Frolic 9

III   Herein of Evalyn Walsh McLean (and her diamonds), Ezra Pound, F.D.R., Robert H. Jackson, and Walton Hamilton 33

IV   Social Philosophy 49

V   The "Loyalty" Cases 61

VI   Antitrust 103

VII   On Insanity and Obscenity and the Law 129

Index of Names 141

PREFACE

It has been the custom in the law firm of Arnold, Fortas & Porter to prepare a file of the letters written in the office and to circulate them among the entire staff. Accordingly, it became my privilege after joining the firm to read several of the letters of Thurman Arnold. I soon became convinced that others might also enjoy reading them. In addition, I was mindful that on June 2, 1961 Thurman would celebrate his 70th birthday. It occurred to me that a little volume collecting some of his hitherto unpublished letters written since he entered private law practice in 1945 might be a most appropriate birthday present. My partners enthusiastically agreed and encouraged me to complete the collection in time for publication next June.

In addition to selections from his letters written during the last 16 years, I have included extracts from two of Judge Arnold's briefs. I chose portions of his reply brief in the Supreme Court of the United States in the "loyalty" case against Dr. Peters, and of his brief in the Supreme Court of Vermont on the subject of obscenity. I also wished to include passages from some of his public addresses; they contained truly priceless gems. Alas, most were delivered extemporaneously; hence, no written record of them exists.

The collection that follows, it must be emphasized, is confined to material written during the past 15 years or so. It is by no means the definitive collection of the wit and wisdom of Thurman Arnold. That must wait another day when a more patient hand may devote himself to collecting and editing all of his letters, opinions, speeches, briefs, books, articles, etc.

The letters in this volume appear just as the author signed them, except that I have omitted a few sentences and paragraphs (indicated by the insertion of dots and asterisks) that did not appear to me to be of any general interest, or that repeated the substance of statements made in other letters included in the volume. In addition, particularly in the sections on the "loyalty" cases and on antitrust, I have omitted a few passages that might needlessly injure reputations or reveal the identity of persons seeking legal advice.

All footnotes are mine unless otherwise indicated.

Victor H. Kramer

Washington, D. C.
February 1961

Foreword

Thurman Arnold — lawyer, legislator, mayor, professor, and judge — has been more deeply concerned with the problems of our age than anyone I know — whether it be the poll tax, segregation of the races, company unions, price fixing, or the war against poverty and illiteracy. He campaigns vigorously in every drawing room, as well as in public forums, for the causes he espouses. He is a versatile advocate; and a dangerous opponent.

I remember years ago a debate on desegregated street cars when Thurman melted the opposition and took the audience by storm with his opening statement, "Letting everyone ride the streetcars will of course produce more revenue. But think how the prestige of the company will be lowered! And after all we are more interested in prestige than in revenue, aren't we?"

Thurman served with distinction as a judge on the Court of Appeals. But he seemed in those days to be caged. His mind was far too active, his interests too wide to find satisfaction in the miscellany of cases coming before a federal court. Practice was his dish; but I think his first love was teaching. His course might be one on Procedure, but he covered during a semester broad vistas of law.

Thurman is in many respects a non-conformist. But he is radical only in the Jeffersonian sense. He is passionately for the individual and passionately against regimentation. He is as truly American as the Rocky Mountains where he was born. He is as rough and ready in his discourse as he is in his appearance. He is not the Georgetown type who complete with boutonniere steps out of a fashion shop. An unfriendly critic once stated, "He looks like he slept in his clothes." He is, however, not unmindful of appearance; it does not preoccupy him. When he walked into his class at Yale smoking a pipe, wearing a hat, and leading his dog, he was not producing an act. He was so lost in thought that the amenities escaped him.

Thurman's humor lightens the serious load he carries. He is not a professional humorist; he is an acute observer and honest reporter. He has a knack of peeling off the false fronts of issues. His casual asides, such as "not all judges wear their beards on the outside," are often penetrating shafts of insight.

He has always enjoyed exploding myths, challenging folklore, scoffing at orthodoxy. His brilliant mind makes him an artist at feats of that character. He eschews false forms. Lawyers often cloak simple ideas in tangled legalisms. Professors, journalists, and businessmen also get caught up in shibboleths and slogans. Thurman has an uncanny ability to tear apart all those tangled skeins and to speak candidly and clearly.

Thurman has many facets. He is stimulating and annoying; calm and excited; conservative and extreme; simple and ingenious. Always he is brilliant. Those who have known him intimately experience an after-glow that makes him deeply loved and highly respected.

WILLIAM O. DOUGLAS

March 17, 1961

I

Personal History

"First, I will tell you a little about myself...."

June 7, 1947

Mrs. Elisabeth Schmidt Ranke
(23) Oldenburg
Parkstrasse 10
British Sector
Germany

Dear Betty:

* * * *

First I will tell you a little about myself. I resigned from the United States Court of Appeals in Washington, D. C., about two years ago because I found the work of a Judge much duller than that of an advocate. I think I might have liked the trial court but on the appellate court we sat in groups of three and all we did was to listen to argument and write opinions. I felt that a more active life was more to my taste, and so after much indecision I finally resigned and went into practice with Mr. Abe Fortas, who had just resigned as Under Secretary of the Interior, which is a Cabinet office. Recently Mr. Paul Porter, who was head of the Office of Price Administration and later a special Ambassador to Greece on an economic mission, has joined our firm. We have five younger lawyers with us, as you can see from this stationery.

Frances and I live in Alexandria, Virginia, which is just twenty minutes from Washington, in a house on top of a hill with about three acres of ground. It is a nice place and Frances likes to raise chickens.[1]

---

[1] This house was sold in 1959 when the Arnolds purchased the Lafayette house in downtown Alexandria, Va.

I suppose Betty has written to you that my sons are both married and going to Law School—one at Yale University and the other at the University of Chicago.

My Mother is about eighty-seven years old and is very well. She lives by herself in Laramie, Wyoming. We have tried to induce her to come to Washington and stay with us but she says that she is just too old to pull up roots and prefers to stay in Wyoming, although that is over 2,000 miles from Washington. However, I get out to see her occasionally.

* * * *

I remember so clearly the last time I saw you in 1910. It seems hard to believe that that was 37 years ago. I remember getting off the train in Breslau and getting to your house early in the morning, too early to get in. I remember how well you played the piano and how charming and lovely you were.

We are very lucky here in America to be comparatively untouched by the two great wars that swept over Europe. I was in France in the Field Artillery in the first war and both of my boys were in this war. The older one was in the Navy, in Europe; the younger one was in the Marines and saw action in the Pacific. Neither one of them was hurt.

Today in America many people are afraid of another war, this time with Russia. However, I am optimistic. I don't believe that anyone is going to be able to plan our ways through the 20th century but I do believe that it is going to be like the 19th century, a century of tremendous progress. The very fact that everyone is afraid of another war is a hopeful sign to me. Wars do not occur when all the world fears them.

The times remind me of what I read about the Reformation when the cement seemed to fall out of social institutions and the world was in confusion for a long time while new institutions were building up. I firmly believe that they are going to build up the same way in the next century.

All this is of little comfort, however, to someone who has to live the next five years in Germany. However, you have my best wishes and sympathy.

Frances sends her very best.

Your cousin,
Thurman Arnold

October 17, 1945

Mr. Joseph Hergesheimer
82 - 102nd Street
Stone Harbor, New Jersey

Dear Joe:

I am probably the worst correspondent in the world but I have an excuse. Since I got off the Bench life has been so hectic that I have not had an opportunity even to take Sundays off. We have had a great deal of business to take care of, it has been impossible to obtain stenographic help or build up an organization, or answer my correspondence. Anyway, this is the best excuse I can offer for not returning your book.

Frances has been doing over a two hundred year old house, of very modest dimensions compared with your famous project. However, during the process of living with the plasterers I have reread "From An Old House" and thought of how much fun I would get out of it if I only had your temperament.

Unfortunately I was brought up in the West and lack the reverence of the past which I should have. And so, I would rather read "From An Old House" than follow its program.

Last night I started to reread "Ballsand" and got as far as the end of Part I before I went to sleep. It seems to have even more charm and vigor and grammar than when I read it first. I don't know anything finer in literature than that first part. Tomorrow night I am going to start in on the second part and I will probably like it just as well.

I may neglect my duties in answering correspondence and returning books, but I am still one of those who consider you our greatest novelist. If anyone challenges this assertion in my presence it will lead to hostilities, which will not be called off even if all the lovely women in America fall down all the stairwells simultaneously.

                                          Affectionately,
                                          Thurman Arnold

                                          March 1, 1946

Mr. John C. Hamm
Route 1, Box 40
Anaheim, California

Dear John:

It was a great pleasure to hear from you again but I was distressed to learn that you have been an invalid. I hope that this letter finds you well and happy. I am sure your heart will last a long time, even on two cylinders, if you take care of yourself and don't put it to any strain.

The new generation of Arnolds is out of the Navy and the Marines, respectively, and starting separate establishments. . . .

* * * *

Both of my sons are going to be lawyers. George is attending the Law School at the University of Chicago. He has gotten an apartment there and is taking his bride to Chicago just after the honeymoon. Thurman is already ensconced as a student at Yale Law School. After they get through they will probably come into my office or some office in New York. But here again I think they will miss something by not going through the country practice.[1] The trouble with the country practice today is that the monopolies have drained the small towns of all their independent industry, leaving only collections and divorces for the lawyers. And so I suppose it's wise for the boys to go to the cities. I am hopeful that the new technical revolution is going to have a decentralizing effect and make the small independent community grow up again.

I enclose a copy of a pamphlet I wrote for the Public Affairs Committee entitled "Cartels or Free Enterprise", in which you may be interested.

I am having to leave for New York in an hour and so I will ask my secretary to sign this letter for me.

Affectionately,

Thurman Arnold

---

[1] Thurman Arnold, Jr. is presently engaged in the private practice of law at Palm Springs, California; George Arnold is in private practice in Los Angeles.

II

Whimsy and Pure Fun and Frolic

"The term 'equestrian statue' means a statue of a great man sitting on a horse. . . ."

January 5, 1959

Dear Charlie and Dorothy,[1]

I have your letters, both of which indicate that you two need legal advice.[2] The proper way to have written, in my opinion, would have been as follows:

Dear Thurman:

We acknowledge receipt of the liquor. It shows a commendable sense of obligation on your part, which we appreciate. However, in all candor I think it is my duty to point out that according to a rough estimate of the liquor you have consumed on our premises, after deducting the amount that a normal person would drink, it would clearly indicate that you owe us at least six bottles more. If you care to send this amount as a birthday or 4th of July present, all additional liquor we receive from you will be treated as a pure gift.

I am proud to know a judge who has a certificate of merit from a bar association. The only thing of that character I got for Christmas was the degree of L.O.M. (Lewd Old Man), conferred on me by my wife because of my constant study of the magazine *Playboy* necessary in order to adequately prepare a brief in its defense before the Supreme Court of Vermont.[3]

---

[1] The Hon. and Mrs. Charles E. Clark. Judge Clark, of the U. S. Court of Appeals for the Second Circuit, was Dean of the Yale Law School while Thurman Arnold was on the faculty.

[2] The Arnolds had sent the Clarks a case of liquor at Christmas. The Clarks wrote at length, profusely thanking the Arnolds and giving other news concerning Judge Clark, as appears in the reply by Thurman Arnold.

[3] See p. 135, *infra*.

I am happy that your portrait is being painted but I consider it far less than what you actually deserve. I have, therefore, formed a committee and am presently engaged in soliciting contributions for a bronze equestrian* statue of you to be erected in the vicinity of the Supreme Court with its rear end to the Court, and the inscription "Charles E. Clark, In Memory of the Eagle Lion Case".[1]

Now, for the more important part of the letter. Frances and I would like for you to stay with us if possible. If that is inconvenient can you reserve us a date for a dinner party?

Affectionately,
Thurman Arnold

January 12, 1948

Dean Wesley A. Sturges
School of Law
Yale University
New Haven, Connecticut

Dear Wes:

Thanks for your note and I appreciate your interest in my welfare.

You asked for suggestions. I would like, if it can be arranged, to have a brass band at the station and a parade of the Governor's footguard or whatever you call it preceding

---

*The term "equestrian statue" means a statue of a great man sitting on a horse. [Footnote in the original letter.]

[1] See *Eagle Lion Studios, Inc.*, v. *Loews', Inc.*, 248 F. 2d 438 (C. A. 2 1957), *aff'd by an equally divided court*, 358 U. S. 700 (1958). Judge Clark filed a dissenting opinion in this case.

me to the Law School. I would like to have the faculty lined up outside the Law School in appropriate robes and a large and expensive present, to which the faculty should contribute pro rata based on their salaries, given to me with a speech by yourself and papers with footnotes and citations by other members of the faculty.

As to my stay, I hope that you will enforce rigorously the rule that there is to be no liquor served in the dormitories.

With best regards.

Sincerely,
Thurman Arnold

June 17, 1948

Mr. Edwin M. Martin
Farnsworth Television & Radio Corporation
Fort Wayne, Indiana

Dear Cousin Ed:

The Capehart arrived. My wife went into an ecstatic tailspin and began to corner the market on records to the serious impairment of our cash position. The machine responded magnificently and played everything we fed it with great skill and virtuosity until an unfortunate incident occurred which hurt its feelings and caused it to go on a sit-down strike.

The fault was mine. I ought not to have expected such an aristocrat among musical instruments to play cheap and inferior records. I did not, however, realize at the time the psychic qualities of your product since you have not seen fit to advertise them. I think, however, that you have something here which your publicity department should be able to use in order to increase your sales among discriminating people. The thing happened in this way.

We tried out La Boheme which the machine digested with great enthusiasm. I then stuck on one of my favorite boogie-woogie pieces. The machine promptly bit a circular chunk out of the edge of the record. This should have warned anyone of any sensitivity but I had had a couple of drinks and failed to grasp the delicacy of the situation. I put on Tristan which the machine played superbly. Then I made my fatal mistake. I put on a record of one of my own speeches over Town Hall of the Air. The machine quit cold. It not only refused to play the speech; it has refused to play anything of any kind since my speech was fed to it.

This is not a complaint. I admit that the machine was right and my own conduct was inexcusable. If you insist on a great opera singer doing a strip tease you're going to get in trouble and I should have known this.

However, the problem is what to do next. I have apologized but it didn't do any good. I have offered to bargain collectively with the machine and even read the Wagner Act to it without any response whatever.

After some thought I think I have hit on a solution. What the machine needs is a couple of drinks of good scotch which I am sure would put it in a mellow and more reasonable frame of mind. My difficulty is that I can't find out where to pour the liquor in. Your instruction book says nothing about it. However I cannot imagine that a company headed by your distinguished self would consent to the manufacture of a machine that would refuse a drink. I am sure that if I put a bottle of scotch, a bottle of fizz water and a glass on the record changer in the right position the machine would mix itself a drink and swallow it. Will you please wire me instructions exactly how this should be done.

My partners think that not having a M.I.T. education I disturbed the machine mechanically. I am willing to try our their theory and have a man come out and look at it. However, I refuse to abandon my own psychic for any such crass materialistic explanation of the machine's conduct.

Your cousin Fanny sends her best wishes and her keenest appreciation. She is sure that the passage of time will cure the Capehart's hurt feelings and that it will soon be its own jolly discriminating self again.

With best regards,

Sincerely,
Thurman Arnold

February 15, 1949

Philo C. Calhoun, Esquire
88 Main Street
Bridgeport, Connecticut

Dear Phil:

I got your letter with the enclosure which I promptly turned over to Mr. Justice Black as you suggested. He has been in the hospital ever since.

I think it is a little early for you to expect me to be writing thank you notes for Christmas presents. I usually try to get these things attended to by June, but February is out of the question. However, since you have raised the issue, I am authorized to inform you that the ashtray came. I find it the most wonderful ashtray I have ever had. I have no doubt that it cost a small fortune, but it is well worth it. I do not agree with you that it does not look like an ashtray. Both my wife and I spotted it for what it was almost instantly. Visitors who come into the house point at it and say, 'That's an ashtray, isn't it?" and I say, "Yes, it's an ashtray." The thing in the middle is to knock the ashes out of your pipe without injuring the delicate adjustment of that complicated smoking tool.

Thanks over and over and over and over again for the wonderful ashtray which you sent me on Christmas and which I have received with gratitude and have enjoyed every moment since its arrival.

Thank you for your thoughtfulness. Thank you for your generosity. Thank you for your discrimination in selecting the one gift which I like more than any other gift I got this Christmas and which, indeed, I like better than any other gift which I got at any other Christmas during my life and which to sum up, I like better than anybody ever liked any gift given to them anywhere or any time.

Affectionately,
Thurman Arnold

May 25, 1950

Honorable Harold H. Burton
Supreme Court of the United States
Washington 13, D. C.

Dear Mr. Justice:

I regret that I am unable to accept your quitclaim deed to the letter addressed to me as Justice of the Supreme Court of the United States and received and opened by you. I realize that this puts on you the burden of getting this man out of the mental institution in which he now resides, and I would like to be of some assistance. My counsel, however, advises me that if I accept your quitclaim to the letter I will be arrested for impersonating a Justice of the Supreme Court of the United States, in all probability convicted, and then on appeal you would be unable to sit.

This would mean that my conviction would be upheld 4 to 4. I just can't take a chance.

With best regards,

                            Sincerely,
                            Thurman Arnold

                            May 18, 1951

MEMORANDUM: Partners, Associates, and Staff of Arnold, Fortas and Porter and their Heirs and Assigns forever.

FROM: Thurman Arnold

The Department of Health and Sanitation of the District of Columbia is about to indict the firm of Arnold, Fortas and Porter for conditions of chaos, disorder, and general litter in their offices which the Department alleges are a menace to health and safety and an affront to the aesthetic sensibilities of the entire population of the District, which the last census shows to be nearly a million people.

The Committee on Un-American Activities has informed

me that the office looks like the kind of an office in which Communists congregate and multiply.

For these reasons I have given Miss Dorothy Bailey the responsibility of raising sufficient hell with everyone from the partners up, to the end that the papers, gadgets, files, books, brief-cases and other flotsam and jetsam which are now scattered around the place from hell to breakfast shall be removed and the semblance of order restored and continuously maintained during the balance of this year of our Lord, 1951.

More specifically, Dorothy Bailey is directed to remove the files which Paul A. Porter has placed on the floor of the library. She is directed to inform Paul A. Porter that the reason we put shelves in the library was to keep things off the floor, an idea which might automatically occur to a more reflective mind. She is further directed to inform Walton Hamilton that the disreputable looking file which he keeps on the floor of the large room must be removed to a less conspicuous site, preferably in his own office although he may keep it in the men's room if he finds it more convenient.

The so-called Conference Room is to be re-arranged according to more adequate aesthetic principles. In this connection I offer the strong suggestion that the couch is a singularly inappropriate piece of equipment for any purposes for which the said conference room is intended to be used.

No one seems to remember to close cabinet doors. It will lighten Miss Bailey's task greatly if anyone who opens them will immediately thereafter close them again. This technique may be difficult at first, but, like riding a bicycle, once acquired it is never lost. It is also a very beneficial exercise which I hope may tend to reduce the weight of some of the heavier members of our little group. The same observation holds for books left on the library table. Replacing them after use creates better circulation of the blood and improves one's metabolism.

The partners, associates, and staff may have access at all reasonable times to my own office so that they can observe how a well-kept office looks.

Yours for a better life
in the future,
Thurman Arnold

October 16, 1951

John S. Miller, Esquire
134 South La Salle Street
Chicago, Illinois

Dear John:

Your letter has just the proper touch of humility and recognition of merit which is adequate to induce me to undertake the hazardous enterprise of moving the admission of your partner to the Supreme Court of the United States. Hitherto I have had an almost unprecedented success in inducing the Court to grant the admission of those whom I have undertaken the responsibility of sponsoring. It may be that this has been just a matter of luck but my friends all tell me that it proves that the Court has unbounded faith in my judgment as to who should be and who should not be admitted to that select little coterie known as the Supreme Court Bar. I would therefore have reasonable anticipation of success, which is illustrated by the betting odds in the office which are 8-to-5 that I get your partner in.

However, I think we should take no chances with a matter as important as this. Will you, therefore, ask your partner meticulously to observe the following instructions:

(1) He should wear a full dress suit, white tie, and a large chrysanthemum in his buttonhole. This will single him out from the less imaginative applicants.

(2) It is important, and I wish you would particularly emphasize this, that he appear in a reasonable state of sobriety. This business of having to prop up the applicants for admission whom I introduce so that they will not fall flat on their faces while I am making my opening statement is quite unnerving.

(3) While not absolutely required I think it would be helpful if he carried with him a large American flag and have a copy of the Chicago Tribune sticking out of his hip pocket in order to rebut any inference that he is a Communist.

Tell Mr. Overton to drop by the office about 11:00 o'clock on Monday, October 22nd, and we will go over to the Court.

Affectionately,
Thurman Arnold

April 7, 1952

Mr. J. A. Livingston
c/o Philadelphia Bulletin
Philadelphia 5, Pennsylvania

Dear Joe:

I have a letter of July 6, 1951, on the letterhead of "J. A. Livingston", signed by some character named "Joe", which I assume to be you. It says:

"Dear Thurman:

This is just to confirm our wager. You are betting me $100 to $50 that the Court of Appeals will reverse in toto the judgment of $2,588,919 against Otis & Co.

My spies inform me that the New York Court of Appeals has just reversed the Otis case and remanded it to the District Court with directions to enter a judgment in favor of the defendant.[1] This makes Otis & Co. solvent again. I hope it does not make you insolvent.

Actually I do not consider that you have lost anything. In fact, I think you have won. The reason I think so is that you have learned the value of a lesson that whatever I say about a law suit inevitably becomes true. You can thus utilize my legal predictions, which I will sell to you at a moderate sum of $50.00 apiece, to make a fortune betting on the outcome of law suits. So, please send me the $50.00 in payment of the debt and another $50.00 for an advance tip on any law suit you name.

There will be no charge whatever for time spent in writing this letter.

With best regards,

Sincerely,

Thurman Arnold

---

[1] See *Kaiser-Frazer Corp.* v. *Otis & Co.*, 195 F. 2d 838 (C.A. 2, 1952), cert. den., 344 U.S. 856 (1952).

January 28, 1954

Mr. Lewis M. Dabney, Jr.
Attorney at Law
165 Broadway
New York 6, New York

Dear Lewis:

It doesn't make any particular difference to me, but if it is convenient with you I suggest February 28th because I'm getting anxious to get started on our trip.

While I don't drink myself I have no objection to your having some whiskey, ale and beer on board for strictly medicinal purposes. I am informed that there are a great many snakes in the tropics and that the liquids you mentioned should be taken both before and after being bitten. You can never tell when some snake will swim out from shore and climb on to the boat. You may insist that this is unlikely, and perhaps it is, but at my age in life I simply can't afford to take chances.

I also concur in the idea of snake dinners.

With kind regards,

Sincerely,
Thurman Arnold

May 6, 1955

Dear Dorothy:[1]

I am in deep trouble and I need your help. Don't leave me waiting at the church as you did so long ago.

The facts are these: Frances gave a dinner party last night

---

[1] Mrs. Charles E. Clark.

for Bill Douglas and Mercedes.[2] Everything went fine until I went to sleep. When I woke up the guests were all gone and Frances was in bed. I got up very early this morning, very quietly, and thought that I could escape comment by getting my own breakfast and leaving. It didn't work. Before I could get away Frances appeared in the doorway and started shooting rockets, atomic bombs, artillery. I think she also had a flame thrower with her, though I am not sure.

I defended myself the best I could. I said that it was customary for great men to go to sleep at parties, citing the Senior Judge of the Second Circuit, Charles E. Clark, as an authority on the subject. She said, "Charlie never goes to sleep at his own parties. He is always a good host. If you want to go to sleep at other people's parties, I do not mind, but you can't go to sleep at the parties I give for your friends".

I don't think this is a sound distinction. I think that His Honor's example is a good one and justifies my own action. I haven't convinced Frances, however, and I am sitting here debating whether I should go home or get a room in a hotel.

Will you please write Frances immediately and tell her that you think she is completely unreasonable, that you have had experience with the same sort of phenomenon. Tell her, if it is true (and I hope it is), that Charlie has not only gone to sleep at other people's parties, that he has gone to sleep at his own parties, and that this sort of relaxation does no harm to anyone.

The older I grow the more disappointed I get in women. You support them, feed them, buy mink coats and automobiles

---
[2] Justice and Mrs. William O. Douglas.

for them, all your life. And then, in your declining years they turn on you like a wildcat. Outside of yourself, the only really gentle and lovable women I have ever known I have read about in books.

Hoping that you will immediately dispatch a reprimand to Frances, I remain

Affectionately yours,
Thurman

Mr. Benjamin M. McKelway July 31, 1958
Editor
The Evening Star-The Sunday Star
Washington 4, D. C.

Dear Mr. McKelway:

On my return from Europe I have your letter enclosing the amusing exchange of correspondence which was certainly a voice out of the past. I am making a copy for my own files and sending the correspondence to Harry Truman.[1]

---

[1] This exchange of correspondence in 1941 between Thurman Arnold and Benjamin McKelway related to an article in The Star entitled "Truman to Talk on Forum". Immediately adjacent to the article was a photograph of Thurman Arnold. Following the publication of the article with accompanying photograph, Thurman Arnold, then Assistant Attorney General in charge of the Antitrust Division, wrote Mr. McKelway on March 29, 1941 as follows:

"Senator Truman has asked me to represent him in a libel suit against the Washington Star on account of the enclosed clipping. He asks for $10,000,000.00 damages but is willing to accept an immediate settlement of $1,666,666.66.

"In estimating the amount of his damages he consulted with Mr. Joseph Padway, General Counsel of the American Federation of Labor. Mr. Padway's only comment was 'Senator, I am astonished at your moderation'."

I note that you ask for my advice with respect to your suggestion of rolling back seventeen years and starting over again. In spite of my unfortunate experience seventeen years ago in attempting to collect money justly due from The Star, I have studied your suggestion and am prepared to advise you.

My opinion is that the whole idea is unsound. Any trained analytical mind brought to bear on the issue you raise would immediately conclude that it might be disastrous for either one of us to turn back seventeen years and start over again. We would make twice as many mistakes as we did on the first round. Indeed, we would both be lucky if we did not wind up either in jail or in the alcoholic ward of some hospital. This is the problem as I view it from the practical angle.

From a legal point your idea presents even more serious difficulties. In the first place it is unconstitutional. It takes property away from your heirs or legatees without due process of law in that it delays their expected inheritances for at least seventeen years. In the second place it is not only an unfair labor practice but also unfair competition with your junior editors.

In my view if you do not immediately abandon your suggested plan, you will be fined by the National Labor Relations Board, ordered to cease and desist by the Federal Trade Commission, and declared unconstitutional by the Supreme Court of the United States. Your only recourse in that event would be to escape to Arkansas under cover of darkness and ask the Governor to protect you with his National Guard. No doubt he would do so but the publicity would be so bad for The Star as to cause it to totter or at the very least wobble in spite of its solid foundation.

I therefore seriously counsel you to abandon the whole project.

Sincerely,
Thurman Arnold

August 6, 1958

Mr. Benjamin M. McKelway
Editor
The Evening Star
Washington 4, D. C.

Dear Mr. McKelway:

Your letter of August 4 was so eloquently persuasive that I abandoned my former position and started to turn the clock back. Unfortunately, however, the plug which I had inserted in the year 1941 was defective, and broke. I was unable to stop the machine until we were both back in the middle of the Eighteenth Century. I know this is not what you wanted but maybe you will find the assumption of the privileges and obligations of an Eighteenth Century gentleman both exciting and interesting.

August 6, 1758

Sir:

I have reread your letter. Even if you actually had any reasons which justified or even palliated the dispatch of such a missive I would not be interested in hearing them.

My seconds will call at your office at 10:00 a.m. tomorrow.

I trust that you will not deny me the satisfaction which under these circumstances one gentleman owes another.

I am, Sir

Y'r obed't serv't,
Thurman Arnold

Mr. George Dixon January 15, 1959
The Washington Post and Times Herald
Washington, D. C.

Dear George:

I seek your advice.

Early this week I was at my favorite hotel, the Biltmore, in New York. I ordered for breakfast grapefruit, eggs and coffee. The waiter inquired "Toast?" I replied "No toast." The combination of two eggs, grapefruit and coffee was listed on the regular breakfast for $1.70. When my check came it was for $1.80. I called the waiter and asked the reason. He said "You ordered a la carte". I said "I thought I was ordering the regular breakfast". He said "No, the regular breakfast has toast on it and you didn't want any toast".

To my legally trained mind this reasoning appeared so eminently sound that I accepted it without protest. However, the next morning I was careful to order toast. The waiter brought it and took it away untouched. The check was for $1.70.

Legally my position, I think, is unassailable. But an ethical problem arises. Is it fair to the Biltmore, my favorite hotel, to make them process, convey and return to the kitchen toast which I have no desire to eat just to save me 10¢. Wouldn't it be the manly thing to do to send 10¢ to the Biltmore and an additional 10¢ for their trouble in preparing the toast which I did not want? The question troubles me. I turn to you because, as a moral philosopher, no one has been your equal since Confucius.

Anxiously awaiting your reply, I am

Sincerely,
Thurman Arnold

January 26, 1959

Miss Ann S. Bujalski
Permissions Department
Yale University Press
New Haven 7, Connecticut

Dear Miss Bujalski:

I have a letter from Professor Sanford Kadish, of the University of Utah College of Law, calling my attention to the charge made for a quotation from my SYMBOLS OF GOVERNMENT which I am informed is now out of print. It appears you want $10.00 for reprinting a couple of pages in his casebook.

This seems to me a most short-sighted policy on the part of the Press to make a charge to a professor writing a book on which there will be no profit. You should be happy to have the Press quoted in a work designed for teaching in a University.

If you insist on making this charge please charge it to my account. I am writing Mr. Kadish to that effect.

Sincerely,
Thurman Arnold

February 16, 1959

Mr. Chester Kerr
Secretary
Yale University Press
New Haven, Connecticut

Dear Mr. Kerr:

I enjoyed your letter very much. You compliment me on my "charm and candor". I am ready to raise that ante because your letter shows more than charm and candor. It has a touch of genius. May I explain?

A less imaginative publisher on receipt of my offer to pay on Professor Kadish's account would have reasoned in this way: "If the old fool is vain enough to pay out $10.00 just because somebody in a cow college is willing to quote from his book, I don't know why I should not accept it". A more imaginative person, perhaps irritated at my criticism, might have written a sharp reply to me.

The touch of genius which you exhibit comes from your sending copies of your letter to me to both Professor Kadish and his publisher, Little, Brown. You have certainly put this fellow Kadish in his place, and if he is still intransigent Little, Brown is going to land on him like a ton of brick. After all, the Yale Press is educational in purpose. It has a moral responsibility to see that outsiders live up to both its economic and ethical ideas.

I have no doubt your letter will do a great deal of good out in Utah. I particularly like your comment that if Kadish is writing a casebook not expecting to make a profit out of it "he ought to have his head examined". As a matter of fact, that's what these fool professors are doing all the time. With respect to my own casebook, which I wrote because I wanted to teach my own instead of someone else's materials, the royalties did not nearly cover my out-of-pocket expenses. If you succeed in inducing scholars not to write except for profit you will relieve this country of thousands of tons of very dull literature. It might well be that this would materially cut down the lists of practically all University presses (except of course Yale). But that would be a bearable misfortune.

May I suggest that you have been unduly restrictive in the very limited distribution of your letter to me which, as we go to press, appears only to have been sent to Professor Kadish and Little, Brown. To get your message across I believe that additional copies should be sent to the Congressmen and Senators from Utah, to the Governor of Utah, to the President of the University, and finally to the head of the Mormon Church.

Hoping that you will see eye to eye with me in this matter, I remain

Sincerely,
Thurman Arnold

February 20, 1959

Mr. Norman Donaldson
Yale University Press
New Haven, Connecticut

Dear Norman:

I have lost my contract on SYMBOLS OF GOVERNMENT. I would appreciate your sending me a copy. My purpose is to buy the copyright, and I am asking what you will take for it.

It certainly can't be worth much to you since you have let the book go out of print and you are not going to get many $10.00 bills from people like Kadish.

If I owned the copyright I have a notion I might be able to keep it in print even if it costs me a little something. This is contrary to Mr. Kerr's philosophy but us great scholars are a peculiar lot, motivated more by vanity than by pecuniary gains.

With best personal regards,

Sincerely,
Thurman Arnold

August 16, 1960

His Honour Judge C. D. Aarvold, O.B.E., T.D.
Foxbury, West Humble
Dorking, Surrey
England

Dear Judge Aarvold:

It occurs to me that the logistics of your arrival in Washington are not properly worked out. I have your car number on the train but I probably will forget it and arrive without the information. In that event I suggest two alternatives:

(1) That you leave the train dressed in your wigs and robes carrying a large British flag. Since it is unlikely that others will have the imagination to do this I can instantly recognize you as you come down the platform. I can further guarantee, if this course of action is adopted, that you will have a front page picture in the *Washington Post*.

(2) If you desire a less conspicuous form of entry and miss me at the platform I will be at the Information Desk with the officials who preside there alerted to point me out on inquiry.

Mrs. Arnold and I are looking forward to seeing you and Mrs. Aarvold.

          Sincerely,
          Thurman Arnold

III

Herein of
Evalyn Walsh McLean
(and her diamonds),
Ezra Pound, F.D.R.,
Robert H. Jackson
and Walton Hamilton

May 22, 1947

Dear Mother:

* * * *

Since I last wrote you—as you no doubt read in the paper—Evalyn McLean died of virus pneumonia. Just when we thought she was getting well she took a turn for the worse and nothing could be done to stop the progress of the disease. Frank Murphy, Cissie Patterson, Frances, myself, Father Walsh, and Frank Waldrop (Cissie's editor-in-chief) were with her when she died.

After her death in the afternoon we had to do something about the jewelry. The stones are worth anywhere from $500,000 to $1,500,000—nobody knows how much because they are completely unique. They were in a wooden box in the bedroom. We made a quick inventory and put them in a cigar box. It was so full of diamonds that it would hardly shut. Frank Waldrop (the editor) and I left in the car. It was Saturday afternoon. We got the vice president of one of the banks down to see if he could take care of the jewels. He called up every bank in town and found that time locks were on; it was impossible to get into any safe deposit box. I was afraid to have the jewelry up in my office. We started going to the big jewelers in Washington who have insurance protected vaults. However, we had no luck there because they said it would void their insurance policies if they took jewelry of that value in without taking out more insurance. So no one apparently would take the jewels. Finally we had a bright idea and called up J. Edgar Hoover. He came down and we sealed the cigar box full of jewels, put it in a safe in the FBI office and Hoover posted a guard over it. On the next Monday we got it out and into a bank vault where it now is.

Frank Murphy and I were appointed executors of Evalyn's estate, but Frank Murphy—because of his position on the Supreme Court—felt he could not act, so I have filed papers to probate the will. She has left the jewelry to be kept until her grandchildren reach the age of twenty-five years when it is to be distributed. It seems a queer will but she had reasons for most of the things she did. In any event, no one could talk her out of it.

Frances and I are quite broken-hearted about her death. She was a fabulous character and I don't imagine this town will ever see anyone like her again. Her real income was only a life interest in property left in trust and it all goes to the children. . . .

One of the interesting things was the fact that her will directed her body to be cremated. She also insisted that she be given a Catholic funeral. She was baptized into the Church but never lived a Catholic life; however her father was a Catholic and it was a very real wish of hers to be given a Catholic funeral. It appears that anyone who has been baptized into the Church may die a Catholic if extreme unction is given. However, we discovered that it is inconsistent with the Catholic service to be cremated so we had a problem. The will said she was to be cremated and, of course, that meant that she could not have her wish under the Catholic service. So we came down to the office and looked up law on Sunday. We discovered that in the event there is no objection made a provision in the will as to cremation can be voided by the family. She was, therefore, given a private Catholic funeral. When the newspapers discovered that she was not cremated, reporters pursued me night and day. I managed to shake them off and passed the buck to Father Walsh. He made a very nice statement and everybody thinks we did the right thing.

* * * *

Lots of love,

April 29, 1958

Mr. Westbrook Pegler
King Features Syndicate
235 E. 45th Street
New York, N. Y.

Dear Westbrook:

It was good to hear from you after so many years. I can still recall the pleasant evening I spent with you when I was serving as Assistant Attorney General.

You asked why it took me "so many years" to spring Ezra Pound. The answer is that it took me about a week. I was not called into the case until Friday, April 11, when Robert Frost appeared and asked me to take the case up as a public service. I agreed to do so.

When I studied the case I found to my surprise that no legal action had been taken on Pound's behalf since December 1946. At that time there was an application for bail pending Pound's trial, which was denied by the court. This application did not say that he was incurably insane and, therefore, the decision was probably correct as a matter of law. However,

Dr. Overholser out at St. Elizabeth's told me that for the last five or six years the entire staff agreed that Pound was incurably insane and could never face trial, and also that he was perfectly harmless and should be released. The only justification for keeping an insane defendant who has been indicted for a crime incarcerated is that he may respond to therapeutic treatment, and thus finally be tried, or else that he would be dangerous to society if at liberty. Neither of these elements existed in Pound's case so there was no excuse whatever for holding him.

Frost had seen the Attorney General and believed that a Motion to Dismiss Indictment would not be opposed, so I drew one up and filed it. I couldn't get a commitment out of the Attorney General prior to my appearance in court, but when the case was called the Government conceded to dismissal of the indictment. The whole proceedings lasted about ten minutes.

I can't answer the question why proceedings were not taken sooner. Pound could have been released on Overholser's testimony many years ago. My guess is that Pound's friends thought that writing letters to the Attorney General was sufficient and the effort was not organized. Nobody apparently thought of consulting an attorney until Robert Frost came down like a whirlwind and saw Sherman Adams who sent him to the Department of Justice.

Since you are interested in the case I send you the pleadings. Frost's statement is a gem, particularly the last sentence.

Best regards.

                                      Sincerely,
                                      Thurman Arnold

May 1, 1958

American Civil Liberties Union
170 Fifth Avenue
New York 10, New York

      Attention: Mr. Malin, Executive Director

Gentlemen:

I would like to correct the impression which your Board of Directors appears to have concerning the Ezra Pound case which appears in the minutes of April 14, 1958.

1. You imply that there may have been a deal with the Justice Department to dismiss the indictment in exchange for Pound going back to Italy;

2. You infer that Pound may have obtained privileged treatment because of his prominence;

3. You conclude by saying that you will not issue a public statement that might hurt Pound, implying that if you did issue such a statement it might hurt Pound.

The facts are these:

On April 11, 1958, Robert Frost representing a group of poets asked me to represent Mrs. Pound in obtaining Pound's release. I of course agreed to do it. On investigating the case I found, to my surprise, that Pound could have been released many years ago by habeas corpus, under decisions of the Ninth and Tenth Circuits and the *Greenwood* case[1] in the Supreme Court of the United States, because (1) he was incurably insane and could never be brought to trial and (2) he was

---

[1] See *Greenwood* v. *United States*, 350 U.S. 366 (1956).

harmless to himself and to society. The only justifications for the incarceration of an insane defendant in a criminal case are (1) that he may be cured and thus face trial, or (2) that if released he would be a danger to himself and others. Dr. Overholser's affidavit shows that neither one of these justifications exists in Pound's case. There was, therefore, no justification for holding him. Furthermore, Dr. Overholser believes he was insane at the time of the offense.

I enclose copy of the proceedings which I filed. The Attorney General stated in open court that he consented to the dismissal of Ezra Pound on the grounds that he had nothing to offer against Overholser's testimony, that he did not believe that Pound could ever stand trial, and furthermore if he did stand trial the Government did not have the evidence to sustain its burden of proof that Pound was not insane at the time of the broadcasts.

In this connection I have read Pound's broadcasts in Italy. They show insanity on their face. They start out charging a Jewish conspiracy with Roosevelt to begin a war to avenge the Jews in Germany. They then degenerate into gibberish. The Italian Government took him off the air very shortly on this account, though he himself would probably have been willing to go on forever.

Your suggestion that the Government insisted on his going to Italy is pure nonsense. The Department of Justice has no interest in his leaving the country. My only worry is that the State Department may not give him a passport. Obviously Italy is the best place for him because he can live cheaper there and will not be so conspicuous. But this is Mrs. Pound's wish and not pressure on the part of the Department of Justice.

So far as your suspicion that he may have been given privileges because of his prominence is concerned it is equally unfounded. It was his prominence, coupled with his anti-Semitic utterances, that made it difficult for past Attorneys General to release him. He has been confined for at least seven or eight years beyond the time that there was any legal justification for keeping him.

Sincerely,
Thurman Arnold

August 20, 1957

Mr. Louis B. Cella
305 Home Avenue
Oak Park, Illinois

Dear Mr. Cella:

I have your letter of August 3. You asked me to give some of my impressions of President Roosevelt.

Answering you briefly, I would say that his outstanding quality as an administrator was his ability to move in different directions and to change his policy when change was needed. He could thus reconcile the activities of men of conflicting philosophy and give unity to his administration.

I recall a dispute that I was having with Leon Henderson with respect to bringing an antitrust case which Leon considered might interfere with the national defense. I finally got to the President on the question and convinced him that the suit should be brought. When I was leaving the room he called me back and said, "I am approving the institution of this suit but it's your business to get along with Leon Henderson better." This was typical of him.

Sincerely,
Thurman Arnold

January 7, 1955

Mr. William M. Oman
Office of the Vice-President
Oxford University Press
114 Fifth Avenue
New York 11, New York

Dear Mr. Oman:

I am sorry to be so long reporting on Gerhart's biography of Mr. Justice Jackson. Unfortunately several briefs came due at the time I expected to read it which delayed me.

First, as to the merits of the book. It is well written, it catches the spirit of Bob Jackson, it is easy to read. By all means it should be published.

Second, as to the book's demerits. Jackson was a great advocate; in fact, the greatest lawyer I have ever known. The book says so over and over again. But it does not in any way explain why he was a great advocate. It does not analyze his technique as a lawyer. In the chapter about Jackson as Solicitor General there is no adequate explanation of the character of his arguments or of the techniques he employed or of the results he achieved. If the author is not a lawyer this may be hard to do. But if there is adequate time to examine the briefs and arguments which Jackson made from the technical lawyer's point of view, the analysis of why he succeeded as an advocate would make a much more complete picture of the man.

A more important defect or perhaps the principal defect in the book is the attempt to justify Jackson when he was plainly wrong. This occurs in the chapter on the Jackson-Black controversy. Here the writer abandons all pretense of impartiality and objectivity. He makes Black a creature of expediency whose political stock in trade was race hatred, until he went to the Court, at which time he shifted to a more humane scheme. Nothing could be greater nonsense. He then argues that Jackson betrays no confidence because Black had previously betrayed a confidence. He uses a column of Doris Fleeson as circumstantial evidence of this. He shows that he knows nothing of the relations between Black and Crampton Harris. Nevertheless he insists that Black could not properly sit in the case. He accepts as true all Jackson's statements in his letter from Nuremberg. He quotes a revision of the Statutes with respect to judicial disqualification as if it prohibited Black from sitting in a case where Harris was involved which it does not do.

The chapter is very bad indeed and should be entirely omitted in the interests of both the publisher and the author. Here we have a good book about a man of great qualities. It is not critical or objective but still it is very good. Then in the middle of the book we have a chapter which is extremely vulnerable. It is so controversial that all the reviewers, many of whom are Black's friends, will concentrate on that chapter. The good parts of the book will be ignored. The fact is that Jackson was a great man but a born scrapper. When he got into a fight he was always sincere but about as reliable as Harold Ickes under similar circumstances. I know enough about the facts to tell you that this chapter in its present form is dangerous to the reputation of the entire book. It will bring down tons of criticism. It will obscure everything else in the book. In my own opinion it is entirely inaccurate.

There are other less important incidents in the book which should be deleted. For instance, we are told that when Jackson took over the Attorney-Generalship he found the Department of Justice in a "mess". This again is nonsense. Murphy had his faults as an administrator but in some respects he was a stronger Attorney General than Jackson particularly with respect to his willingness to enforce the antitrust laws. Jackson, an old NRA advocate, never really believed in them. But anyway, why build up Jackson at the expense of Murphy? They were both great figures of strikingly different qualities. What does it add to the book to bring down the wrath of the Murphy admirers, of whom I am one? Why not say something about Jackson the administrator as he was a very good one indeed. Why not analyze the way he administered the Department. All the book does is to say Jackson was a great administrator and Murphy was a mess.

This is a single instance. The book, however, should be gone over carefully for other instances of this kind. It's a good book but I think it would be a better one with the corrections I suggest.

The manuscript is being returned to you by Railway Express.

Sincerely,

Thurman Arnold

[WALTON H. HAMILTON *died on October 27, 1958. At the memorial services on October 30, Thurman Arnold spoke these words.*]

We meet here together to bid a last goodbye to Walton Hamilton. In doing so we have a peculiar bond between us. That bond is the respect and honor in which we hold him.

I have been requested to express here what we all must feel, not because I am adequate to the task but because I was one of his oldest friends. For 28 years I have worked for him and with him, first as his colleague at Yale, then at the Department of Justice, and finally as his partner in the practice of law. To have known Walton Hamilton this intimately is one of the cherished experiences of my life.

He was in every respect a most unusual man. To me he represented the free spirit of inquiry into human affairs. He touched no subject, philosophical or even procedural, without discovering new and unexpected facets which he illuminated alike by his original analysis and his flashing humor. It was as impossible for Walton Hamilton to be dull as it was for him to be pedantic. His mind ranged over every field of economics and law. But the market place—the means by which civilized man, by voluntary and competitive division of labor, makes and distributes goods and thus improves his lot—had a special fascination for him. His restless energy produced a series of books on the mysteries of trade, neither conservative nor radical, but penetrating the very heart of the American market place,—observing the interactions of legal symbols and economic dogma with the pressures of the industrial revolution of the 20th century, which few men understood as well as he did.

These books are more than analysis and observation. They are imbued with a poetic spirit and reverent ideal of the value of the freedom of man, which begins, though it does not end, in the market place. In his last book, written after the age of 75, he expressed his faith in American traditions as follows:

> "In some form or other the rivalry of men will continue to be employed as an instrument of the general welfare. It is not important that the arrangements which currently are set down as the competitive system will endure. It is important that the spirit of competition shall be enhanced and not impaired. There must be an outlet for the creative urge, free play for the dynamic drive. In a society, as in the physical world, motion is inseparable from life."

That was Walton's social philosophy. It was also his personal religion.

Walton Hamilton will be best known for his teaching and writing and his public service. But the young men in our office knew him best as a fighting lawyer. He entered the private practice of the law when he was sixty-five. There he proved to be a born advocate. He loved litigation. He had the resourcefulness and imagination of a born advocate. It was during this period that he learned his sight was going and that he could never read again. His response to this challenge was inspiring. It was the response of a man, young in spirit, who would not even entertain the notion that he was growing old. He provided himself with readers. His remarkable memory came to his aid.

He was soon able to take the lead in a case in California, involving months of trial, long cross-examination of expert witnesses, and the keeping in order and introduction of thousands of documents, all this when he could not read a line on a printed page. To me this refusal to admit defeat was the culminating achievement of his life.

He loved music so much that he actually lived it. By that I mean that in all his writings, in all his speeches, indeed in his arguments before the court he wove together the contrasting themes of his ideas like music, illuminating them with sparkling analogies, giving them the balanced rhythm and the movement which was at the heart of his inner being. He was a happy man because he had that balance between ideals and harsh reality which spells spiritual harmony.

Today on his 77th birthday we bid him goodbye.

IV
Social Philosophy

". . . the most important social values in the world are the things that make no sense."

". . . if people generally agreed with what I said, nothing I said would be any longer true."

October 30, 1957

Mr. Frank C. Waldrop
Hidden Valley Ranch, Ltd.
Elkmont, Alabama

Dear Frank:

It was good to hear from you again, but at the same time quite a surprise. I never had any idea you read *The Progressive* since I don't happen to take it myself.

* * * *

May I ask why you get in such a stew because people in general can't get along without a sharply defined philosophy of government and fall in love with ritual, etc. That's been true for some twenty-five thousand years and it's hard for me to see how organized society can be held together without it. When we get in the state where we don't have to fight over ritual we'll eat without tablecloths and use our fingers instead of silverware. The fact which you do not seem to realize is that the most important social values in the world are the things that make no sense.

As for F.D.R., why don't you read Schlesinger's latest book. It's excellent and if you go over it carefully it may clear up your present state of utter confusion. In the meantime, if you want to improve your mind without the expenditure of any capital, read the reprint of a very great article on Jerome Frank which I enclose.[1] Don't throw it away because it will be only a short time that the demand for it will be so great that it will be a collector's item.

---

[1] The article by Thurman Arnold was published in 24 U. of Chicago L. Rev. 633 (1957).

I note that you do not say anything about integration. That would seem to indicate that you have not yet become a true Southerner. Referring to this subject, I was talking to my friend Charles Pickett, the greatnephew of Pickett's Charge. I told him that I was completely in accord with the Virginia Governor's plan to deny funds to any school which was integrated under a court order. I told him, however, that in my opinion it did not go far enough. He said, "Well I'm glad that at least you're coming to your senses." "Yes," I said, "I have concluded that any funds spent on the education of Virginians are a waste of the taxpayers' money. It has been conclusively demonstrated that education does Virginians no good. So, I think all the schools should be closed, not just the integrated ones." The more I think of this the sounder idea it seems to be.

With best regards and affectionate greetings from Frances to you and your family, I remain

Sincerely,
Thurman Arnold

June 22, 1960

Mr. Sergius M. Boikan
Ames 411
Cambridge 38, Massachusetts

Dear Mr. Boikan:

Your letter of June 16 is most interesting and it is quite clear that you understand thoroughly the point of view which I tried to advance in my book, my articles and teaching. Senator Taft, who was a good friend of mine and a trustee at Yale, used to tell me that he thought it was a good thing to have one fellow like myself on the Yale Law Faculty but he certainly wouldn't want many more of them. There is some truth in what he said. The paradox is that I doubt if any law school as an institution can ever maintain an objective point of view as to the law. It would be like asking the Catholic Church to write an objective history of Catholicism.

Therefore, law schools all over the world gravitate into theology. The realistic law schools build up a theology of their own. If you read Professor . . ., who writes frequently, you will see this process. He was a student of mine and was a convert to my point of view. Now he is caught in the throes of a new jurisprudence which I am unable to understand. My own way of expressing the paradox is to say that if people generally agreed with what I said, nothing I said would be any longer true.

* * * *

Sincerely,
Thurman Arnold

January 22, 1946

Mr. Carl Christ
10 Dickinson Street
Princeton, New Jersey

Dear Mr. Christ:

Thank you very much for your letter about my two books.[1] I am very flattered at what you say.

---

[1] *The Symbols of Government* (1935) and *The Folklore of Capitalism* (1937). See also his book, *The Bottlenecks of Business* (1940).

With regard to a study of the point of view which I express, if my advice is worth anything I don't believe that you need it. There is no science of semantics in any real sense. The human race is not going to change and use words in the future with any more clarity than they have used in the past. I wrote my book as a country lawyer without any knowledge of semantics but simply from my observations of the current scene. I would advise anyone else who wished to take advantage of the same point of view and apply it to study directly the things in which you are interested rather than indirectly to work on any theory of language.

For example, "Folklore of Capitalism" is nothing but a condensation of a series of hearings before the Securities and Exchange Commission over which I presided. I had never heard of the word semantics when I wrote it. I don't know whether this advice will be helpful or not, but in any event I appreciated your letter.

Sincerely,
Thurman Arnold

December 26, 1956

Mr. James E. Titus
Department of Government
Texas Technological College
Lubbock, Texas

Dear Mr. Titus:

I want to apologize for such a long delay in answering your letter. I am flattered that you should spend so much time studying my writings and the questions you put are quite interesting. I will try to answer them.

Question No. 1. Was not your criticism of myths and traditions based on the belief that men must adopt an open-minded, experimental attitude toward social problems?

I think this is probably correct. In spite of my claim to be purely objective there is no doubt that I had a bias towards an experimental attitude rather than one which followed accepted fundamental principles.

On page 269 of *The Symbols of Government* I wrote:

"There are signs of a new popular orientation about the theories and symbols of government which is arising from a new conception of the function of reason and ideals in the personality of the individual. A new creed called psychiatry is dimly understood by millions of people. Popular magazines are appearing, discussing from an objective point of view problems which used to be considered the exclusive property of the moralist. A conception of an adult personality is bringing a new sense of tolerance and common sense to replace the notion of the great man who lived and died for moral and rational purposes. Under these new attitudes men are becoming free to observe the effects of changing beliefs, without the discomfort of an older generation which swung from complete certainty to utter disillusionment.

"Such a conception, once accepted, will in the long run spread to government and social institutions."

The prophecy has proved to be true, yet the new conception of governing people by the manipulations of symbols and attitudes has not brought pleasant results. It has given us Madison Street instead of Wall Street, it has led to the belief of the Communist that he may manipulate men's minds with conscious hypocrisy. It has not been a unifying force and I have now come to the belief that moral principles firmly believed in as a matter of faith are essential to freedom in any society. In times of change they get in our way. But the concept of an adult personality is no good as a religion or a source of inspiration either in government or in personal life. It is too completely materialistic. So, in this respect I have changed.

Question No. 2. Would you agree with Dewey that the task of liberalism is "the mediation of social transitions" which occur when traditional ideas do not square with contemporary facts of life?

Yes, I would agree.

Question No. 3. Do you not consider Holmes and Cardozo as "liberals" primarily because they refused to view the law dogmatically?

I personally would not consider Holmes a liberal at all but I agree that his only claim to that position is what you have stated in the question.

Question No. 4. Would you please explain the thinking behind this statement on page 343 of *Folklore:* [quotation].

You certainly picked out a bad piece of writing. I'll be damned if I know what it does mean. If *Folklore* were in type instead of plates I would strike the thing out. It is one of the most confused sentences I have ever seen.

If you ever get to Washington I would appreciate your calling me and I will buy you a luncheon.

With best regards and hoping to see your paper when it is finished, I remain.

Sincerely,

Thurman Arnold

November 12, 1959

Mr. Thomas C. Wert
443 North Monte Vista
Azusa, California

Dear Mr. Wert:

I am flattered that you should take my books as a basis for your study. With respect to my attitude toward them today, I do not think I would retract anything I said except as to numerous errors in detail which I have no doubt exist. The books of course do not contain any positive philosophy. I still cling to the belief that faith and pride are the most important factors in social organization. It is easy to expose the irrationality of man's conduct and show the tremendous cost in material advancement of our belief in old symbols. Yet that cost must be paid because without them, as we can see in the case of Russia and Germany, men lose themselves in the greatest illusion of all, the illusion that absolute power may be benevolently exercised.

In the last chapter of *Symbols,* on page 269 I note that the psychiatric point of view is spreading to the conduct of government and institutions and express the belief that that attitude toward law and economics "is slowly appearing to create an atmosphere where the fanatical alignments between opposing political principles may disappear and a competent, practical, opportunistic governing class may rise to power". I appear to have been right in my prediction but not in my hope. . .

                                      Sincerely,

                                    Thurman Arnold

June 22, 1960

Mr. John R. Glenn
513 E. 8th Street
Bloomington, Indiana

Dear Mr. Glenn:

Thank you for your letter of June 15. It was a real pleasure to read such an enthusiastic though undeserved tribute, and it is gratifying to know that something one has written has stimulated someone else to think along the same lines.

My anthropological point of view may be useful in understanding human institutions. It will never, however, be an inspirational force. In the concluding chapter of *The Symbols of Government* I express the opinion that the psychiatric viewpoint I have adopted might in the future make society more realistic, practical and humanitarian. Years have passed and I do not find the point of view expressed in my book adopted by Madison Avenue. They recognize that people are motivated by symbols and can be manipulated by them. Having reached this position Madison Avenue thinks it knows how to lead people not only on the advertising front but on the political front. They are successful in inducing businessmen to pay large sums of money to create the proper "image" in the public mind. So far as public influence is concerned, however, Madison Avenue is an absolute failure. Their objective philosophy is too completely materialistic.

The paradox was best expressed by my friend Harry Sullivan whom I invited to give a course of lectures at Yale to a seminar group. He spent three lectures, full of apt illustrations, convincing the students that they should become adult and rise above their infantilisms. He described the necessary process of adjustment. At the end of the last lecture he paused and said, "Now, young gentlemen, when you have lost your desire for adventure, when you have forgotten romance, when the only things worthwhile to you are prestige and income, then you have grown up, then you have become an adult". The students left the lecture in utter confusion, but I know of no better way of expressing the reason why it is impossible for any society to become truly objective.

I have read your very able article in the *Indiana Law Journal* and have given it to Mr. Fortas. It is a superb analysis and one of the most interesting that I have ever read.

With best regards and hoping that you will drop in to see me if you ever come to Washington.

Sincerely,
Thurman Arnold

V

The "Loyalty" Cases

"Everyone here who can investigate is investigating. Everyone who can't investigate is being investigated. Our firm is trying to do its part in the conflict."

{The following is an extract from a Statement by United Public Workers of America (CIO) as amicus curiae in support of a Petition for Rehearing in the Supreme Court of the United States in Friedman v. Schwellenbach. The Statement was filed in April 1947, signed by Thurman Arnold, Abe Fortas, and Milton V. Freeman. See 330 U.S. 838 (1947); 331 U.S. 865 (1947).}

But this assault on freedom of opinion will not stop with Government employees. Assaults upon freedom have a habit of growing beyond a stated objective. They quickly attack not merely a manifestation, but freedom itself. So this crusade, once under way, will not stop with its victims in the federal service. It will spread and is now spreading over this country, blighting our democracy and bringing fear and distrust to American homes throughout the nation.

January 7, 1947

Professor Edward S. Corwin
Princeton University
Princeton, New Jersey

Dear Corwin:

Thanks for your letter. I appreciate your comment on my talk.

... I am convinced that the activities of the Rankin Committee are a dangerous threat to civil liberties ...

My point, as you apparently understand, is that no committee or administrative tribunal or court may seize the private papers of an individual on the sole ground that they consider that his activities may be found to be "subversive and un-American." It seems to me that the term "subversive and un-American" can only mean what the particular individual likes or dislikes. For example, I would call anyone who advocated any form of cartel organization "subversive and un-American." Yet, that would scarcely justify a tribunal investigating people who had opinions contrary to mine, if such investigation went to the point of seizing private papers.

There are some difficult distinctions which I must make. For example, I would permit the investigation of any form of organized political activity, Democratic, Republican or Communist, because political organization is a subject matter for legislation. I would further permit the subpoena of papers from any financial organization on the ground that finance is a subject of legislation. However, where a group of individuals is engaged in distributing relief to Spanish refugees and has conformed to all the requirements of the State Department regarding the collection and distribution of the money, there is no ground for seizing their papers on the charge that many of their members are communists.

The position of the Rankin Committee appears to be that if a group is suspected of Communism, their relationships with their friends and their charitable contributions may be investigated on that ground alone. They go so far as to say that since Communism is a dangerous philosophy, all persons suspected of Communism are subject to search and seizure.

I must distinguish between this and the investigation of the political activities of communists. Certainly they should show all their contributions to such organized activities, but because the opinions of a group happen to be regarded as "subversive and un-American" should not give jurisdiction for investigating their activities unless they are shown to have some connection with political or financial organizations.

The difficulty, of course, is the fixed belief that whatever communists do is a dangerous thing and all of them must be up to something. If this be a principle in American law it means that a Congressional Committee can select any group of opinion which it considers un-American and segregate those who hold such opinion out for special investigation to which other Americans are not subject. This is a dangerous threat to civil liberties whether the Supreme Court sustains my position or not.

Best regards.

Sincerely,
Thurman Arnold

November 3, 1947

Honorable Robert A. Lovett
Acting Secretary of State
Washington, D. C.

My dear Mr. Secretary:

In answer to your letter of October 31 in which you refuse to permit certain individuals discharged from the State Department for security reasons to resign, I would like to call your attention to certain important facts to which I do not think you have given sufficient consideration.

In June 1947, the Department of State announced in a press release that ten employees had been dismissed for security reasons. On July 3 the Secretary of State elaborated on this release by a statement that these employees had been indirectly associated with representatives of foreign powers. The names of these individuals have since been published. The Department has also given information to prospective employers, one of them a university, that it has a reasonable doubt that these men are good security risks.

So far as I know, the publication of such accusations against members of the staff of the State Department without specifications and accompanied by the statement that evidence will be withheld is unprecedented. It is idle to say that these accusations are not an attack on the character of these individuals. Everyone who reads the accusation is bound to believe that in the opinion of the State Department these men are tainted with communism. Indeed, the only purpose of your Department in giving nationwide publicity to these accusations was to prove to the public and to Congress that the State Department is zealous in getting rid of persons whose undivided loyalty to the United States could not be depended upon.

As you know, the inevitable result of these accusations thus publicly released is to impair and indeed probably to destroy the ability of the accused individuals to make a livelihood, particularly in academic life, a career which most of them have chosen. We can discover no way that these individuals can answer these charges.

The precise issue raised, therefore, is whether it is proper for a great government department to publish the most damaging statement which can be made about an American citizen today, to wit, that he is disloyal to his country or tied up in some vague way with a foreign power, without giving him a chance to be confronted by the witnesses against him. This we say is a violation of the spirit of the Bill of Rights.

You say in your letter that perhaps he may appeal to the Civil Service Commission. But the injury was done by public release of the State Department and no other department can correct that injury. Further, the Civil Service Commission has informed us that unless you permit it to reveal the evidence against these men, it will be unable to allow them to defend themselves in the traditional American way. And according to your letter, the evidence can never be disclosed. Under these circumstances, what kind of a hearing can the Civil Service Commission give?

Your defense as is stated in the Department's letter to a prospective employer, is that "when a reasonable doubt is raised as to whether the continued employment of an individual would constitute a security risk, it is the policy of the Department to resolve such doubt in favor of the government." Assume the necessity of such a policy. Does it mean that a reasonable doubt about the reliability of an individual justifies the Department in accusing him and at the same time withholding the evidence which is the basis of your accusation? This is what the Department has done.

The purpose of the State Department in ridding itself of suspected members of its staff is fully served when such men terminate their employment. We had not thought that it was the duty of the Department to pursue such men into private life with unproved accusations. But, if indeed, the Department has such a responsibility, the least protection which should be given is to give the accused individual opportunity to defend himself against those accusations and to be confronted with the witnesses who make them. Your officials have admitted that such accusations may be untrue since they are not tested by a full hearing. The accused individuals are no longer in your employ. Why then should accusations be made against their loyalty when the Department is unwilling to accord them a hearing?

We earnestly request that you change your present policy of pursuing them into private life with charges against which you give them no opportunity to defend themselves.

We repeat, we are not asking you to continue these men on your staff. We are only asking that they be given a hearing in an American way or else that they be permitted to resign. Surely one or the other of these alternatives should be open to them. Surely such a policy will give the maximum freedom to the Department in the control of its staff. All you will lose is the opportunity to spread accusations you are unwilling to prove against men who are willing and anxious to leave your service.

We would appreciate your further consideration whether the Department desires to exercise such a privilege in view of the obvious dangers to civil liberty which it carries with it. We respectfully repeat our request for a personal conference with the Secretary.

Sincerely yours,
Thurman Arnold
Abe Fortas
Paul A. Porter

October 17, 1949

Honorable J. Howard McGrath
The Attorney General of the
    United States
Washington, D. C.

Dear Howard:

I have been encouraged by some of your recent statements which clearly indicate your desire to keep the loyalty program from becoming an oppressive injustice on government employees. It is in that connection that I address this letter to you.

We represent Dorothy Bailey in a case which has caused wide comment....

Briefly stated, the point I wish to make is this: The President's loyalty order states its intention to secure maximum protection to the Government and equal protection to the accused. The standard it sets up is that the findings of reasonable ground for belief that the accused is disloyal must be made "on all the evidence". The Department of Justice is contending and indeed has succeeded in getting Judge Holtzoff to hold that a secret report undisclosed to the accused constitutes "evidence" under the terms of the President's order.

It is difficult for me to believe that the President would desire his order to be so construed or that you, as the Attorney General, would desire the Department to take that position in court. The use of a secret document as evidence in the Dorothy Bailey case seems to us identical with the use of a secret document in the famous Dreyfus case. The tribunal which convicted Dreyfus acted on the contents of a sealed envelope handed to it by the Ministry of Justice. This was in 1894. In 1899 the case was reopened because the conviction had been obtained on that sort of evidence and Dreyfus was given a new hearing. The only difference between the Dreyfus case and the Bailey case apart from the penalty involved is that there was *some* open evidence against Dreyfus. There is none in the record against Dorothy Bailey.

It is also difficult to distinguish the practice used in convicting Dorothy Bailey and the practice condemned in the trial of the Nuremberg judges by an American military commission. It is of course true that the secret reports made the basis of the

German convictions were utilized in criminal trials whereas Dorothy Bailey is deprived of her job by an administrative procedure. However, the President's order requires the conviction to be on all the evidence and his own commission has said that the use of secret documents as evidence is "a final degradation of justice".

We, therefore, urge you to examine this case with great care to determine whether you want to exercise the weight of your great office in urging in effect that what was wrong for German judges to consider as evidence was nevertheless intended to be included by the President in the administrative hearings which he instituted by his order. To advocate such a practice seems to me contrary to every American tradition of justice.

The case will be commented upon for years to come. Whatever the result it will be a landmark in American civil liberties law. For these reasons we think the case should be called to your personal attention. . . .

With kind regards,

                            Sincerely,
                            Thurman Arnold

                            April 19, 1950

Mr. George K. Gardner
Langdell Hall
Cambridge, Massachusetts

Dear George:

                   *   *   *   *

Washington today is in a state of hysteria which you wouldn't believe unless you were here. The fantastic cloak and dagger intrigue, the bribery which we suspect surrounds the Lattimore case, is unthinkable. It is getting so attorneys are afraid to handle these cases for fear of losing respectable clients. The senators will tell you privately what they think of it but don't dare come out publicly, with rare exceptions. And the tragedy of it all is that I have very good grounds to believe that it is the communists themselves who are turning in to the FBI and the Congressional committees accusations against persons who are in their way. There are positive indications that this is what happened in the Bailey case. Dorothy Bailey was attempting to take a non-communist position in a situation where the communists in the union were trying to get control. Everybody in the union knows who the FBI agent is. She attends all the secret meetings with a notebook. She is a very naive person who makes a wonderful conduit through which the communists can get rid of people they don't want, using the government agencies as a weapon.

The communists are able today to paralyze our thinking about foreign policy. It takes about six months for anyone to be cleared for the State Department. If he ever had an original idea or was interested in the problems of communism they are afraid to use his services. Thus they are pursuing their stupid policy with respect to China partly because they were afraid to agree with Lattimore who is the world's greatest expert on the subject. This reaches down into all the minor posts. All government affairs are becoming a dark secret. Government personnel is deteriorating to an alarming extent.

I hope the Supreme Court will have the courage to act, but I am not encouraged by their past record in certiorari cases of this character.[1] However, this case does give them an out. All they need to do is to interpret the President's order according to its plain intent and they can disregard the constitutionality of the loyalty program. This in itself would do a lot of good. The extent of the fear is indicated by a very nice government official of long standing whom I met for the first time at dinner. A lady asked him about the Lattimore case. He blushed and said "I have no comment to make on it either way".

In the face of this atmosphere [Judge] Edgerton is showing real courage. He is liable at any time to be subject to a speech in the Senate investigating communism on the Bench, and he knows it. The un-American Activities committee is already extending its investigations to communist influences in the District of Columbia. It recently summoned a business man of liberal leanings whom I represented. He was cleared or at least not questioned again. But the fact that he was called became known and his business suffered. His summons before the committee was like a summons before the Spanish Inquisition except that their methods go only to the destruction of the business and reputation of the victims.

* * * *

Sincerely,

Thurman Arnold

---

[1] The reference is to *Bailey* v. *Richardson,* 182 F. 2d 46 (C A D.C. 1950). The Supreme Court affirmed the decision of the Court of Appeals against Miss Bailey because of an equal division among the Justices, 341 U. S. 918 (1951).

June 1, 1951

Lawrence Bogle, Esquire
Cassius E. Gates, Esquire
Bogle, Bogle & Gates
6th Floor Central Building
Seattle 4, Washington

Gentlemen:

* * * *

I take this occasion to report to you on the Washington situation. We are engaged in a number of great civil wars. Everyone here who can investigate is investigating. Everyone who can't investigate is being investigated. Our firm is trying to do its part in the conflict. Yesterday we got provisions through the lines to a gallant group of beleaguered bookies who were beseiged by the Kefauver Committee. This morning, at great personal risk, we laid a wreath on the tomb of the unknown crapshooter. (You will understand we cannot give the location of this grave for security reasons).

You in your peaceful community have no idea of the added peril occasioned by General MacArthur's decision not to die but just to fade away. Heretofore we had associated the process of fading away with quiet gardens in autumn. We now know it is a new explosive comparable to the atom bomb. The worst is not yet over. It is rumored that ten other generals are beginning to fade. If they fade in succession life for the next few months will be unbearable. If they fade all at once there will not be a house left standing. We have therefore stationed a vigilance squad at the Pentagon with instructions to remove to an open field and detonate any general who shows the slightest signs of fading. This is difficult and dangerous work. I am not sure it is constitutional. But stern necessity demands it.

Under these difficult circumstances, I am entrusting this letter to a secret agent who will try to sneak it through the lines so that you may have an expression of the admiration of myself and my partners on the twenty-fifth anniversary of the founding of your firm.

Sincerely,
Thurman Arnold

March 25, 1952

Mr. Robert M. Hutchins
Associate Director
The Ford Foundation
914 East Green Street
Pasadena 1, California

Dear Bob:

Thanks for your letter of March 21. I appreciate your willingness to discuss the Paraguay project.

I am glad you are interested in civil liberties. In my view there is only one way they can be protected at present, and that is to have a responsible organization willing to enlist the services of counsel to protect individuals whose opinions and past associations are being scrutinized by Congress. The standards of acceptance of cases would be the ones that we have adopted—(1) full disclosure of all relevant facts to the Congressional Committee, and (2) the right to withdraw representation if any material fact has been misrepresented.

At the present time the situation of anyone charged with Communist activities, however innocent he may be, is very precarious. Mr. Lattimore is a good example. He has not the means to defend himself or even to pay for the transcript of the proceeding. We of course take his and all other cases for nothing and, if necessary, put up expenses, but the burden on an individual firm is very great. There are very few lawyers of standing willing to take these cases. As an example of this I cite the case of . . . who has been asked to appear before the Committee. He wants us to represent him but we can not do so on account of a possible conflict . . . The policy of the McCarran Committee is to first have the witness in secret session, get him to testify to the best of his recollection as to events from five to ten years ago, then bring him on at a public hearing, ask him if he did not so testify at the secret session and then show him some letter to which he has not previously been given access which shows that he is wrong. This then is branded as an untruth. The McCarran Committee long ago gave up all idea of proving Lattimore was a Communist. Instead they spend weeks of time in trying to catch him up in contradictions and give the impression that he is an evasive and untruthful witness.

In this situation we are trying to get counsel for. . . . He is entitled to be represented by a man of responsibility and standing. We have not been able to find a single lawyer who will take his case.

It seems to me that there should be some organization of unimpeachable responsibility which can employ counsel so that they may avoid the onus of appearing on behalf of someone suspected of Communism. This is a real burden, as we ourselves have found out. The same thing applies to the President's loyalty program.

Just a few days ago a professor at the University of . . . , with only a small salary, came into the office. A year ago he was asked by the War Department to teach in their staff college. He got a leave for six months from the University, it was extended at the War Department's request for six months. He is about to return to . . . [his university] next week. He is suddenly served with questionnnaires and asked if he wants a hearing. His trouble was that he during the years 1943 to 1946 was head of an adult education program involving employment of lecturers all over . . . [his State]. Some of the lecturers are now suspects, and hence his loyalty investigation. His preparation for this hearing involves a great deal of work, examination of documents, the minutes of the Lecture Committee of the University of . . . . If he resigns and goes back to . . . [his university] without a hearing the fact that he was not exonerated may be held against him permanently. He cannot afford the expense of retaining counsel in addition to the necessity of his going back . . . to dig up the evidence in his favor. We have taken his case on but there is a limit to the number of cases any one firm can handle.

There is an urgent need for some organization to protect the kind of people I have mentioned.

                                          Sincerely,

                                      Thurman Arnold

February 3, 1953

Mr. Joseph Hergesheimer
Stone Harbor
New Jersey

Dear Joe,

I appreciate your sending me a copy of the New Leader.

I have been terribly busy on the Lattimore case. The indictment is a document which is new in American jurisprudence and if it is sustained, we are in a bad way regardless of how the case comes out before the jury. When a man is tried for his sympathies, it having been charged that he is sympathetic with Communism, and he has to go back through his entire life and writings to show he isn't, as against excerpts torn out of context, none of us is safe.

Affectionately,
Thurman Arnold

March 14, 1953

James Lawrence Fly, Esquire
Fly, Shuebruk and Blume
30 Rockefeller Plaza
New York 20, New York

Dear Larry:

I will briefly review my difficulties with the American Civil Liberties Union for your information at the next meeting. There is nothing confidential about this letter and you may show it to anyone if it suits your purpose.

My fundamental complaint may be stated as follows: I do not think that the American Civil Liberties Union should intervene in any case where the defendant has adequate counsel without either a request on the part of defendant's counsel or the consent of defendant's counsel if the Union desires to make an offer of assistance. In cases where the defendant is not represented or inadequately represented a different principle might arise.

I was, therefore, surprised to learn from Baltimore some time ago that the Union had considered the question of filing a brief amicus curiae without consulting this firm and had turned it down. I was naturally concerned about this because every conceivable story is being ferreted out and used against Lattimore and because I did not want to see a headline in the paper to the effect that the American Civil Liberties Union saw no question of civil liberties in the Lattimore indictment. I, therefore, got in touch with Mr. Firman (or he got in touch with me, I've forgotten which), and as a result I had a conference with Mr. Firman and Mr. Levy. It was apparent that our ideas were so different that any brief amicus curiae written by the Union would contradict our position. I told Mr. Levy about my fear of publicity. He agreed that the Union should drop the whole matter, and left me with that understanding.

The next time the matter came up was when a member of your Baltimore chapter came to see me expressing surprise that I didn't want the Union to file a brief. I told him the reason was that any brief reflecting the Union's position would hurt us. I asked him to convey this to the Baltimore chapter. He said that the Baltimore chapter was indignant and he could not predict the consequences of a meeting which was about to be held.

The next time I heard of the matter was when Mr. Firman

arranged a conference held with Senator O'Mahoney and myself on Thursday, March 12. I had before me the minutes of March 3, 1953, of the Due Process Committee which outlined the scope of the brief. The Committee proposed to file a brief arguing "that either the indictment should be dismissed *or* a bill of particulars should be furnished in sufficient detail to remove the vagueness of the first count." We pointed out that this was not our understanding of the proper procedure; that we were going to argue the motion to dismiss first and that the bill of particulars would not be relevant until that motion was decided. We also said that the words "sympathizer" and "promoter" of "Communist interests" were so vague that no bill of particulars could possibly be filed which would change the nature of the count, and finally that the Union would at least by inference be supporting the Government's position as to the validity of the indictment. We were shocked at this notion that no civil liberties were involved and did not want such an idea suggested by a brief amicus curiae.

With respect to the other counts we were in equal disagreement. For example, in the second count it is alleged to be material whether or not Lattimore "knew" that a man named Chi was a Communist. Lattimore testified that no one *"told"* him that Chi was a Communist. When asked when he "learned that Chi was a Communist" he said that he had learned from the newspapers that he had *taken service* under the Chinese Government, later stating that this did not necessarily indicate that he was a Communist as they were taking many non-Communist experts at the time. After these questions were asked the Senate Committee defined the term "Communist" to include anyone who furthered "Communist" purposes. Then Lattimore

79

was charged with perjury for saying "he knew" that Chi was a Communist "in that he had been *told* that he was a Communist". The Union report came up with the following gem:

> "It was agreed by the Committee that the definition of 'Communist' was immaterial in this count, since it makes no difference what a Communist is if Lattimore had in fact been told that Chi was a Communist; and, therefore, that no civil liberties problem arises on this point."

To illustrate the absurdity of this position I informed Mr. Firman that every single member of the Due Process Committee was a Communist under the definition of the Committee. I then said "From now on if you deny that they are Communists under oath you will be committing perjury because you have been told they are Communists and your acceptance of the definition or disagreement will make no difference." He laughed and I am sure saw the point. I cite this only as an illustration, and will not burden you with an analysis of our equally violent disagreement on all the other counts.

Whether I am right or wrong in my position it is clear that there is no possible meeting ground between ourselves and the Union. I am aware of the pressure on the Union to placate its Baltimore chapter and at the same time to maintain its position that an indictment such as Lattimore's does not violate due process. But I insist that the ethics of our profession require that where an accused is represented by competent counsel no outside lawyer should seek to present views to the court which counsel for the accused thinks will hurt its case, particularly when those views are ostensibly advanced in defense of the accused. I also think that the Union was abusing its position when it held hearings on the merits of our motion to dismiss as a civil liberties issue and broadcast them in mimeographed form knowing as it must that in a cause celebre such information is bound to leak.

I trust that you will be successful in preventing a situation where we will have to publicly object to the filing of a brief amicus curiae.

This is the second draft of this letter. The first one was longer and I tore it up which may or may not be circumstantial evidence of how I really feel.

Sincerely,
Thurman Arnold

October 29, 1954

Mr. Herbert Monte Levy
Staff Counsel
American Civil Liberties Union
170 Fifth Avenue
New York 10, New York

Dear Mr. Levy:

Apparently I have not made my position clear to you in connection with the American Civil Liberties Union's participation in the Lattimore case. In the first full paragraph on page 2 of your letter of October 28th, you state that your Committee considered whether American Civil Liberties Union could join in a motion to dismiss the new Lattimore indictment on First Amendment grounds, as amicus curiae.

I am a member of your national committee. I have in the past supported the American Civil Liberties Union. I don't want you in the Lattimore case. If the American Civil Liberties Union attempts to participate in the case as amicus curiae or otherwise, I will object strenuously. I repeat, I want the American Civil Liberties Union to stay out of this case.

I thought that the position that you took with respect to the first count of the old indictment, insisting that the correct procedure was to demand a bill of particulars in lieu of filing a motion to dismiss, was wrong and was an unwarranted attempt to interfere with the conduct of the case by Senator O'Mahoney and this office. I was confirmed in my opinion as to the strategy of the case by the District Judge and by eight judges to one in the Court of Appeals[1] and by the Solicitor General, who refused to apply for certiorari. But whether we were right or wrong, in our judgment the threat that the American Civil Liberties Union might interfere was highly objectionable.

I have seen some of the letters that have emanated from American Civil Liberties Union's office about the Lattimore indictment. I don't like them.

Your present letter is a resumption of the kind of quibbling debate which ignores the fundamental legal and constitutional issues, and violates the fundamental civil liberties values that are concerned. I have no patience with your approach, and no time to devote to dealing with it.

If the American Civil Liberties Union management does not realize that the new indictment of Owen Lattimore is a fundamental assault upon civil liberties, it will certainly be beyond my capacity to demonstrate the point. Beyond this, the technical questions of law and the questions of legal procedure

---

[1] See *U. S.* v. *Lattimore,* 112 F. Supp. 507 (D. C. D. C. 1953), *aff'd,* 215 F. 2d 847 (C. A. D. C. 1954).

should, I suggest, be left to me, Abe Fortas, Paul Porter, and our partners and associates.—and to Senator O'Mahoney when he returns to participate as co-counsel in the case.

At your request, I send you under separate cover a copy of our Motion to Dismiss. I have no doubt that you will disagree with it as you did with the Motion to Dismiss the old indictment, but I have no intention this time to engage in a debate with you. The only thing I want is for the American Civil Liberties Union to stay out of this case.

Sincerely,
Thurman Arnold

June 19, 1953

Honorable H. M. Kilgore
Committee on the Judiciary
United States Senate
Washington, D. C.

Dear Senator Kilgore:

I have been so busy trying cases in the last month that my correspondence has gotten far in arrears. I apologize for not answering your letter of May 21, 1953, with respect to a proposed amendment giving Congress the power to grant immunity to witnesses before Congressional Committees.

I would be very much opposed to such a measure. The temptation on the part of a Congressional investigating committee to act as a sort of roving grand jury is very great. Certainly they should not have added to their authority the power to get public statements from witnesses which would inevitably reflect on other persons not before the committee by promising freedom from prosecution to the persons who made such statements.

With kind regards,

Sincerely,
Thurman Arnold

December 2, 1954

Mr. Peter V. Ritner
Feature Editor
The Saturday Review
25 West 45th Street
New York 36, New York

Dear Mr. Ritner:

Thank you for your letter. Apparently you know how to get on the blind side of authors. Of course I was greatly pleased by your reference to "The Folklore of Capitalism".

But to get back to the fundamental differences between us. This is where I think that you and apparently my friend Zech Chaffee are wrong. Once you admit that the present congressional investigation is instituted to expose the views and associations of individuals to the public is a debatable question, you have lost the cause of free speech. This admission has the same destructive effect as if the Episcopal church allowed its pulpit to be used to debate the divinity of Christ. When churches have tried something like this they become weak and ineffective. The idea of free speech and of fair trial is a spiritual value which is irreparably damaged when its advocates admit it is debatable and strive to present both sides.

The particular cause of my irritation over the telephone was caused by the following statement which I quote from the Morris article:

> "The sincerely disassociated and contrite ex-Communist is a more informed person generally on the issue of Communism and generally has acquired antibodies against further infection. They are of inestimable value as a source of evidence . . ."

When I think of the stable of ex-Communists kept by the Committees and the Department of Justice willing to perjure themselves at the drop of a hat, and then when I see you treat a statement such as the above seriously, I blow up with a loud bang emitting suffocating fumes.

I have no doubt this is "liberal censorship" but I'm for it. We need more of it.

I enclose for your perusal an article which I just wrote for The Pocket Book Magazine with the hope that you read my aspirin story on page 38.

Best regards in the zealous hope that this letter saves your immortal soul, I remain

          Sincerely,
          Thurman Arnold

          February 4, 1955

Mr. B. M. McKelway
Editor, The Evening Star
Washington 4, D. C.

Dear Mr. McKelway:

I appreciate your spending so much time answering my letter. Our difference seems to be a different set of values with respect to the First Amendment. Prior to the Lattimore case

I would have thought that almost anybody would have agreed that the sincerity of a man's appraisal of his own views,—his opinion whether or not they were unduly sympathetic with Russia,—could [*not*] be the basis of a perjury charge. If they could there would be an end to opinion testimony. Hypocritical opinions are expressed at every hearing. Hypocritical speeches are made in every campaign, and few newspapers are able to avoid coloring their expressions of opinion to fit the financial situation in which the paper finds itself. Should they be asked whether they are sincere and put to a jury trial on this issue?

May I put it this way. If the First Amendment does not protect a man who gives an economic or political opinion from indictment on the ground that he was insincere the right of free speech is clearly in danger. For example, I was charged with bringing antitrust indictments for political purposes. I denied it under oath. Even if I had been insincere it would be far better to let it go than subject me to indictment. Take your own letter. Had you given it under oath men who agreed with me that your observations about Judge Youngdahl were unreasonably critical could have convicted you for perjury if the prosecutor whipped them up into disliking you or distrusting you. And of course today in the present state of hysteria the hardest man to defend is one who has been accused of Communist sympathy. Juries have believed the ridiculous tales of professional perjurers like Matusow in this kind of a case.

And so when you say that Judge Youngdahl was on shaky ground in applying the First Amendment I am profoundly shocked. And the fact that the Court of Appeals who applied the First Amendment in the Rumely case did not apply it to Lattimore does not reassure me.

Again, when you criticized Judge Youngdahl for his condemnation of the United States Attorney in the affidavit of bias and prejudice I was also shocked. Never before has a responsible government official filed an affidavit which stated that the official written opinion of a judge can be used to show bias and prejudice. If such affidavits can be filed by the Department of Justice without reprimand the pressure on Federal judges would become unsupportable. I have a clipping service and have been reading the editorials commenting on Youngdahl's dismissal of the indictment. There are many like the New York Daily News with millions in circulation which has editorially demanded that Youngdahl get off the bench and take his seat with the defense. These pour into our office. Large numbers of people actually believe the United States Attorney is right and that Youngdahl's decision in favor of Lattimore is a dishonest one. In all conscience how can the Star support this kind of tactics on the part of the prosecution? Why should we be compelled to try a case with a judge under that kind of pressure? Why should not such tactics be reprimanded?

Well, anyway the Star's recommendation has been accepted and the Government has decided to appeal. The five years of persecution go on. The appeal probably will not be heard until next Fall. Lattimore, once a prosperous citizen consulting large corporations on Eastern affairs, making money out of his writings, is excluded from the Johns Hopkins campus. His capital is dwindling. His reputation is still good abroad. He has been invited to speak at an international conference in

Rome. He probably can't get a passport. He has been offered a small position in Baltimore which might make him a living. They are unwilling to take him, however, until the criminal proceedings are ended. Meantime the struggle goes on to get funds to meet the costs of this litigation. Fortunately he does not have to worry about attorneys' fees. There aren't going to be any. And your paper has editorially stated that it is fitting and right that this continue another year.

Will you pardon me, therefore, if I express my disappointment and shock that the Star should have lent its support to keeping Lattimore on the grill and expressed the opinion that he should be forced to trial for the utter impertinent trivia which remain.

I know that you are an honest and sincere man. And the Star is unquestionably a great paper. That is why my disappointment is so keen.

Sincerely,
Thurman Arnold

May 10, 1955

Hiram C. Todd, Esquire
Mudge, Stern, Baldwin & Todd
40 Wall Street
New York 5, New York

Dear Mr. Todd:

I find on my desk this morning your letter of April 21, 1955, which I thought I had answered; at least I intended to. I do not find any record of an answer. Therefore, I must have neglected it. Please accept my sincere apologies.

I certainly applaud any action with respect to the loyalty board hearings. My own belief is, however, that there is no possibility of conducting such hearings in a fair way. Take the Oppenheimer case, for example. Unlike Dr. Peters, Oppenheimer was confronted with the evidence against him. It did no possible good. The reason is that there is no such thing as a fair trial of a man's character. These trials of course are trials not of what a man has done but what he might do because of tendencies. A stigma is put on him with the appearance of a trial.

There is no possible sense to this. Non-Civil Service personnel can be discharged without any explanation. Civil Service personnel are only permitted to explain; they have no right to a hearing. The discharge is simply for unsuitability.

This has worked well enough in our Government until the present hysteria. I think that fair procedures in such cases would make them even more unfair. The whole hearing system should be abolished and the old Civil Service rules reinstated. The employees should be screened but if they fail the screening tests there should be no publicity of why they were relieved from their jobs.

You may be interested in our Reply Brief filed in the Supreme Court in the case of *Peters* v. *Hobby*.[1] I enclose a copy.

Sincerely,
Thurman Arnold

---

[1] See *infra*, pp. 92-101.

March 19, 1954

Chester T. Lane, Esquire
Beer, Richards, Lane, Haller & Buttenwieser
150 Broadway
New York 38, New York

Dear Chester:

* * * *

One case which we are taking up to the Supreme Court of the United States may interest your Committee. It is the case of Dr. John P. Peters who is a professor in the Yale Medical School and a distinguished public health man. Peters at the request of the Government had been a consultant on public health, coming down to Washington perhaps once a year for a few days. Loyalty charges were brought against him, the record is one hundred percent in his favor, Judge Clark and ex-President Seymour of Yale were among those who testified for him, not a line of derogatory testimony can be found in the entire proceedings. He resisted discharge on account of disloyalty only because he did not want to have that kind of a charge against his name and he did not think he could afford to resign. The evidence on which he was found to be a loyalty risk was not disclosed. No one has the faintest idea what it is. He has been declared ineligible to serve the Government in any way for three years. The legal situation is as follows: The case offers an opportunity to get the Supreme Court to review the Dorothy Bailey case, a case which we took up some years ago. The cases are almost identical excepting that Dorothy Bailey was a high paid civil servant in the United

States Employment Service. Her job was not sensitive and she had access to no information excepting regarding employment. The long record which we built up at her loyalty hearing shows that she never followed the party line, never joined any subversive organization, voted against Wallace, etc. Yet on a secret dossier which she was never permitted to see she was discharged as disloyal. We sought a declaratory judgment in the District Court which was dismissed. The Court of Appeals, two-to-one, affirmed the lower court; the Supreme Court of the United States affirmed the Court of Appeals four-to-four. We now have a new Chief Justice and that is the reason we are willing to take the Peters case up.

The idea that a man can be penalized as a near traitor and declared ineligible to serve his Government on evidence which he has never seen is so shocking that perhaps your Committee might be interested. What these cases need more than anything else is some conservative support. The principle involved in this case is most important. If the Supreme Court would only compel the Government to disclose to the accused the evidence against him it would correct most of the present abuses. This of course would only apply to non-sensitive jobs because in sensitive jobs no hearing is necessary.

If the principle involved in the Peters case is of interest to your Committee I would earnestly solicit that they study it. I enclose a copy of the complaint filed on behalf of Dr. Peters.

          Sincerely,
          Thurman Arnold

{The following are extracts from the first section and the entire Conclusion in the Reply Brief for Petitioner in Peters v Hobby, filed in April, 1955, and signed by Thurman Arnold, Abe Fortas, Paul A. Porter, and Milton V. Freeman. See 349 U. S. 331 (1955).}

I
THE ISSUE

From reading the government's brief one gets the impression that the issue in this case is whether the courts may interfere with the selection and removal of government personnel. The Attorney General appears to think that the elaborate inquisition called the loyalty and security program with its hierarchy of trial and appellate tribunals, with its army of informers, with its periodic announcement of new totals of victims, is an incident of ordinary personnel management and therefore beyond the protection of the Constitution.

It is our position that proceedings under the loyalty program are not a part of routine personnel management; and further, that the government's power with respect to its personnel is subject to constitutional limitations in certain situations.

Wieman v. *Updegraff*, 344 U. S. 183, establishes the latter point; that the constitution is applicable to the government's power to dismiss employees. *Wieman* holds that the Government may not discharge employees for prohibited reasons— that is, on the basis of arbitrary and "indiscriminate classifications".

The issue in the present case is whether the constitution also applies to the dismissal of an employee for disloyalty, after a formal hearing. The answer to this, we believe, must be in the affirmative. The government may dismiss employees for such reasons as it chooses, limited only by such constitutional considerations as *Wieman* v. *Updegraff* illustrates. But where the reason for dismissal is alleged disloyalty, and where the Government purports to determine disloyalty by means of a formal hearing held pursuant to elaborate regulations, the basic requirements of due process must be observed.[1]

* * * *

Never before either in times of war or peace has the government resorted to anything remotely resembling the loyalty program ... Neither has any such program been adopted by industries which are far closer to national defense than the Department of Health, Education and Welfare. Nor has any labor union sought to protect itself from infiltration of Communists by setting up this kind of a formal inquisition. They have solved their problems with Communists quietly and efficiently without spreading fear and distrust throughout their organizations.

The General Electric Company is a vast organization deeply involved in national defense and in the possession of government secrets. It is a far richer field for Communist exploitation than is the field of public health. In the tumult and shouting that has accompanied the loyalty program the heads of that company found it necessary to reassure their employees that they had no intention of establishing a loyalty program to judge men's qualifications by presenting the testimony of secret informers to boards of prominent citizens selected from Who's Who.[2] General Electric repudiated this notion as a function of

---

[1] [Footnote omitted]
[2] [Footnote omitted]

management. It said that private employers "cannot and should not be expected to embark privately upon sweeping programs for judging the loyalty of employees" because the "government, not private citizens, must identify traitors—and that this government duty could not safely or properly be left to private citizens." A. A. Berle, Jr., *The 20th Century Capitalist Revolution* 91 (1954).

The truth of these statements is obvious. No rational employer would believe that he could promote efficiency by employing an army of secret informers, by collecting gossip, by staging hearings which precluded any opportunity to explain and refute, thus spreading fear, confusion and suspicion throughout the enterprise.

* * * *

CONCLUSION

We believe that the only issue in this case is whether the government can stigmatize a citizen as disloyal to his country after a formal hearing without due process of law. The government argues that this is a dismissal case, and professes to see no difference between this case and dismissal on any other ground or by any other procedure. We think that the government itself has recognized the difference by the elaborate regulations and proceedings for loyalty and security cases which it has not seen fit to set up for other types of discharge.

The difference becomes crystal clear when a loyalty discharge is compared in its important and significant particulars with other informal types of dismissal.

1. The loyalty program was publicly proclaimed in E. O. 9835 as a method of "maximum protection" of the govern-

ment from its enemies and at the same time a procedure which gave "equal protection" to the employee from "unfounded accusations". No such pretense is advanced in informal procedure.

2. The loyalty program purports to judge employees on "all the evidence". The informal proceedings make no such promise.

3. The loyalty and security programs set up boards which are independent of the personnel officers who hire and fire. These boards are given great dignity. The Attorney General takes pride in pointing out that the members are in Who's Who (Resp. Br. 103, fn. 46). The accused is promised that the independent judgment of these boards will determine his case. But in every case where a secret F.B.I. report is the basis of the board's decision the accused is deprived of the independent judgment of the board. The secret report on which the board decides is summarized and edited, by the F.B.I. which also evaluates the reliability of the informant. Thus independent judgment of such a report by the board is impossible.

The informal procedure holds out no promise for independent judgment by persons outside of personnel management. No particular dignity or sanctity is given to these judgments by personnel officers.

4. Loyalty and security hearings take as their subject matter the entire life of the accused. They make it possible for the board to exercise hindsight judgment during four periods of history. The first of these periods is the early part of the Russian Revolution which some men hated for its cruelty and its radical philosophy while others thought it was a historical

event which might free Russia from the tyranny of the czars. The second of these periods followed the recognition of Russia by the United States. During that time distinguished men like Ambassador Davies wrote his *Mission to Moscow* which might now easily be taken as evidence of Communist tendencies in spite of the fact that it was an entirely honest appraisal. The third period followed the German-Russian pact in 1939. The fourth period covered the years during which Russia became our ally in the war, our associate in the Nuremburg trials, and our colleague in founding the United Nations. The last is the period of the cold war during which hatred and suspicion of Russia has become so intense that some men think they are entitled to view any opinion of the accused favoring Russia in any of the former periods as cumulative evidence of disloyalty. The persons who initially edit, summarize and determine the relevance of associations and opinions in all these historical periods are agents of the F.B.I. Valuable as the F.B.I. is as a police agency, they are not qualified to be and cannot be objective historians. Indeed, no group of men is less adapted for this sort of task than the police.

By contrast the atmosphere that surrounds ordinary discharge does not compel an exhaustive inquiry and appraisal into a man's statements and associations covering his entire lifetime, or an appraisal in the light of complex historical events.

5. The loyalty board hearings, as we have shown, in actual effect endow the Department of Justice with power over every other agency of government to whom it is authorized to furnish its secret reports. No one, not even an Ex-President of the United States, can have formed an opinion contrary to these

secret reports without risk of a future attack upon his own character as a security or loyalty risk. Under this system a prejudiced Attorney General could impose his prejudices on the personnel of every government department. Mistakes in these reports can never be corrected because they can never be discovered. Nor can malice and bias ever be exposed. No man can be an investigator, accuser and evaluator of his own accusations. Even the most upright cannot escape their own prejudices in the vague area of loyalty and security covering as it does the lifetime of an individual.

The informal procedure may of course lead to mistaken discharges. But this is only an incident to the business of making a living. It is a risk which men must assume in a free society. It is not endowed with solemn sanction of judicial procedure. It does not have the pretense or trappings of a trial and hence does not cloak unjust official action with the apparent impartiality of our trial procedure.

6. Since the formal procedure appears to be a fair trial of men for an offense that is akin to treason those who attack it are linked with the enemies of this country. This is evident from the following testimony of Assistant Attorney General Tompkins on March 8, 1955 before the Senate Sub-Committee on Reorganizations of the Senate Committee on Government Operations:

"It is becoming increasingly clear that the current attack against Government Witnesses and informants of the Federal Bureau of Investigation has its roots in a Communist effort to stem the successful campaign of this Government to eliminate the subversive threat of Communism to our internal security. It has as its objective the hamstringing of the FBI's informant system and there is no more effective way of attempting to do this than through the demand for confrontation of witnesses in these non-criminal matters."

Thus those who argue for confrontation are linked with traitors. No high government official has denounced those who criticize Civil Service regulations as aiding the Communists in their efforts to infiltrate the government.

7. The terrific impact of our formal loyalty and security procedure has been felt over the entire world. In a short period of time it has provided us with more *causes celebre* than our entire system of judicial trials over a quarter of a century. There is the Oppenheimer case, the John Peyton Davies case, the extraordinary Wolfe Ladejinsky case, the spectacle of Dr. Condon being tried and acquitted again and again till he was driven from government and then even from his job in private industry. There are the cases of John Stewart Service, Dorothy Bailey, and finally that of Dr. John Punnett Peters. It is only out of proceedings that have the appearance of judicial process that such public attention can arise.

In contrast all these persons could have been released by an informal procedure with only passing comment. Consultation with Dr. Oppenheimer could have been broken off quietly and without fanfare. Dr. Peters' term could have been left to expire without a formal finding of disgrace. To classify a procedure such as this as a mere incident to the power of dismissal is simply to deceive ourselves. We can be sure that we will deceive no one else.

8. One final element in this procedure is, we think, conclusive evidence that the executive is here seeking to exercise judicial or quasi-judicial power. In this case no conceivable managerial reason existed for branding Dr. Peters disloyal to

his country. Not even the interest of government economy can be urged. No worse test case could possibly be selected.

Why then does the government not reverse the board in this particular case since Dr. Peters' term has already expired, and await some better set of facts to present to this Court? Why does a high Justice Department official give an interview to the press in which he states:

> "The Justice Department wants as much to win public opinion for the Government's loyalty-security program as it does to get a clear-cut Supreme Court decision this year upholding dismissal of Dr. John P. Peters under that program."[20]

The reason is that the Attorney General, as others have done in the past, wants the sanction of judicial process to dignify the executive action in this case. This is a familiar political phenomenon in history. The Russians attempted to satisfy the same desire in their early purge trials of 1937. There was no lack of executive power in the Russian Government to dispose of those defendants without the finality of a trial. But instinctively the Russian executives wanted to dress their acts in seemly judicial clothing. By doing so they were enabled to appear righteous and thus to allay public doubts and misgivings. It also enabled them to deflect public criticism. No one can criticize a state which disposes of its enemies by fair means. Even an unjust decision is protected if the process is fair. It is the same instinctive desire which is back of the defense in the Peters decision.

No doubt the government would have preferred a better test case than that of an eminent senior professor at Yale University with only a casual connection with the government

---

[20] *The Washington Star,* March 28, 1955, p. 4, Col. 3. [ftn in original]

who was vouched for by distinguished men he had known all his life. But the judicial robes in which the government had clothed the Loyalty Review Board forbade its reversal by executive action. Had the government reversed the board by executive action the illusion of independent judicial judgment would have been destroyed. And so the Attorney General has no alternative except to defend the egregious error of this Loyalty Review Board.

If this Court declares the procedure unconstitutional it will have done an inestimable favor to the Department of Justice. This is because history tells us that attempts to obtain judicial sanctity for arbitrary executive acts without the substance of a fair trial blow up in the faces of those who initiate them. This was true in the case of Joan of Arc. This was true in the case of the Russian purge trials. That the nature of the process here is judicial is conclusively demonstrated by the fact that the government, though it has the legal power to do so, cannot remove the stigma from Dr. Peters without seeming to impair the authority of its alleged independent tribunals. This salient fact should remove all doubt that the proceeding here is judicial in character and must be conducted with due process.

Other cases involving government employees may come before this Court which may be in a twilight zone between the managerial and judicial function. But this case does not require this Court to fix with precision the line beyond which the Government cannot go in discharging employees without a fair hearing. If all the considerations which we have discussed above do not push it into the area where due process is required then there is no such line. This government cannot set up a procedure which is essentially judicial with one hand and rob it of due process with the other without violating the Constitution of the United States.

Respectfully submitted,

* * * *

December 10, 1958

Mr. William Clifford
Simon and Schuster, Inc.
Rockefeller Center
630 Fifth Avenue
New York 20, New York

Dear Mr. Clifford:

There must have been some kind of a misunderstanding between myself and Gardner Jackson. I did not agree to endorse Benjamin Ginzburg's book, *Rededication to Freedom,* but only to read it and see if I could endorse it. The book is an eloquent and a slashing attack on about everybody who has been connected with the security program. . . .

If I may make a suggestion it would be that Mr. Ginzburg drop the Hiss trial from the book. Although personally I have never been able to believe that Hiss was guilty it cannot be said he did not have a fair trial or that the appellate court could have reversed the jury verdict on the record before it. To intimate that perhaps Hiss was framed by some Government source is to indulge in the same kind of unprovable accusations that the author complains the committees are doing. The author's treatment of the Hiss case, therefore, makes the book extremely vulnerable to attack. Every critic of the book will point to it as evidence of irresponsibility.

I have read Alistair Cook's fascinating analysis of the case with great interest. I am inclined to believe that he may be right but that is solely because of my personal acquaintanceship with Alger Hiss. People who do not know Hiss or who have not read Cook's book will consider Ginzburg's statements fantastic.

Sincerely,
Thurman Arnold

VI

Antitrust

". . . America can only survive under a competitive philosophy and a strong antitrust enforcement."

October 17, 1945

Mr. Matthew Josephson
R. D. Gaylordsville,
Connecticut

Dear Mr. Josephson:

* * * *

I do not fear . . . the philosophical difficulties you raise in your letter. Of course competitive doctrine is a kind of folklore but so is every other economic theory. In my view it is the only one that we can operate under. It is part of our cultural pattern and no nation can change that pattern.

Of course, it is true that every economy in action will be inconsistent with its ideas. Russia will go capitalistic and independent enterprise will start up in a cartel system in spite of hell and high water, et cetera.

It is equally true that even in a competitive sport like prize fighting a man who gets the heavyweight championship will think that he has worked hard enough for his title, that he has a great investment in it and that he ought not to be compelled continuously to fight newcomers.

All of these forces are always present in every economy. Nevertheless, America can only survive under a competitive philosophy and a strong antitrust enforcement. Lacking that, it will become a subsidiary of some other dominant country. This was proved by the fact that prior to the war we had become an economic subsidiary of England and, to a certain extent, of Germany. We couldn't run the cartel system. It is too foreign to our habits of thought. For that reason Germany made suckers out of our businessmen.

I can put it another way. When we reach a frame of mind

where we can make Owen D. Young the Earl of General Electric and put him in some kind of a governmental House of Lords we will have one of the minimum essentials to a noncompetitive big business bureaucracy which will work at least as well as it works. So long as we can't do that the operation of monopolies in this country will create only confusion, bitterness, and the constant backing and filling which went on during the years of the New Deal.

We are not going to pull out of the present mess without a great deal of confusion. On the other hand, we are not going to get any feeling of economic comfort until our predominant ideal has at least a semblance of reality.

I enclose a copy of a recent pamphlet I wrote which confuses the subject even more than this letter does.

* * * *

Sincerely,
Thurman Arnold

Enclosure: Public Affairs Pamphlet No. 103 "Cartels or Free Enterprise?"

August 1, 1947

Mr. Dexter M. Keezer
Director, Department of Economics
McGraw-Hill Publishing Company, Inc.
330 West 42nd Street
New York 18, New York

Dear Dexter:

Thank you for your letter of June 19, 1947.

Answering your question I believe that by and large antitrust enforcement offers the only chance which the United

States has to preserve a competitive system. Theoretically, there are many other ways of accomplishing the same end. You could arrange a tax system to penalize monopoly. You could limit the size of corporations or regulate the amount of business that they did. For instance, Fred Raymond has worked it all out along these lines in a book, which John Chamberlain endorses, entitled "The Limitist".

The antitrust laws have not been effective in the real world. Therefore, the temptation of an academician is to create a scheme which worked well on paper and compare it with an actually operating law. This seems to me very naive political thinking. My belief is that the only instrument which has a chance to preserve competition in America is antitrust enforcement through the courts. Traditionally we accept the courts as an institution which cannot be criticized or badgered as we badger an administrative bureau. A grand jury investigation can be conducted without public protest in a way that was impossible for an administrative tribunal to function. That is because there is a judge in a robe sitting over it. An administrative tribunal taking drastic action against a powerful political group cannot survive. We have watched the Labor Board swing too far under union pressure and then we see Congress destroying its public prestige and power. Under our tradition and habits you cannot do that to courts.

Unfortunately the antitrust laws depend on the public attitude. It doesn't make much difference what your instrument is, it will not be enforced unless there is a strong demand. There was such a demand when I was in office. Today, in an economy entirely dependent on government spending we are sufficiently prosperous that there is no demand. However, I expect the demand to grow. I give you a single example.

The . . . [Newspaper] abused me for starting the Associated Press suit. Now they are being squeezed by [a newspaper chain] (this is not for public use) who is trying to take away their comics in order to put . . . [a competing newspaper] in a better competitive position. . . . Suddenly these people who attacked the Associated Press suit take a train to Washington and retain me to do something. . . . Of course you can't get the Department to move yet. There is no public pressure and our government is purely political. At the end of our conference I asked the editor of the . . . if maybe he hadn't been wrong and I hadn't been right about the Associated Press suit.[1] He laughed and said there might be something in that.

It is only that sort of pressure which will create antitrust enforcement. My political guess is that we will not depart from the traditional ways of enforcing antitrust laws. They are the most effective because the grand jury is a much better instrument than any ever devised to smoke evidence out. (I think I am being repetitious here but I am in a hurry). Books like "The Limitist" are plausible on paper. Actually, my guess is that is not the way we are going to meet the problem.

Sincerely,

Thurman Arnold

---

[1] See *United States* v. *Associated Press*, 52 F. Supp. 362 (S. D. N. Y. 1943), *aff'd*, 326 U. S. 1 (1945).

April 28, 1948

Professor L. E. Aylsworth
114 Social Science Hall
The University of Nebraska
Lincoln 8, Nebraska

Dear Professor Aylsworth:

I am very happy to answer your letter of April 22, 1948, although my experience has been that it is useless to argue with members of the American Medical Association. I suppose they are no different than any other association such as the dairymen when they attack oleomargarine, or the Southerners on civil rights, or the National Manufacturers Association on a protective tariff, or John L. Lewis on coal. However, I myself have always been a little more irritated with them because the problem of health is involved.

In answer to your first question, of course I warned the American Medical Association and the local medical association and tried to induce them to stop their boycott. They sent their attorneys to me who threatened dire consequences in the event any proceedings were taken against them. They declined to make any change in their practices. During the progress of the suit they conducted a campaign of misrepresentation of the purpose of the suit. Thousands of letters poured into the White House and also to the Attorney General to stop the proceedings. Pressure was also put on the medical schools. For example, two professors at a prominent medical school had urged the commencement of the action. When I called on them to testify they said that they did not dare, that it might hurt their school and their positions in the school.

In answer to your second question, of course no one in

his right mind expected that the American Medical Association would not fight the Wagner Bill. In so far as there was intimidation it was the other way. There were numerous threats against the Administration and some people in the government were successfully intimidated by the Association so that they attempted to stop the suit. Fortunately, however, the President did not listen to them.

I never had any question about the illegality of the restraint of trade in the American Medical Association case.[1] The Association relied on a statement of Holmes' in the *Baseball* case[2] to the effect that medicine was a profession and not a trade and tried to build up from this their right to boycott organizations which did not follow their code. Apparently they were sincere in the belief that the court would hold their way and, as you remember, they did get a lower court to dismiss the indictment. After the Court of Appeals had reversed the case I am inclined to doubt whether the attorneys themselves thought they had much chance except through jury oratory. They retained my friend Bill Leahy, who is one of the best jury lawyers in the United States, and he did get the individual doctors off by pleading with the jury not to convict "your doctors and my doctors". The verdict was illogical in that the jury found that the Medical Association had violated the Sherman Act but that no human being had had a hand in that violation. However, it is the function of a jury to be illogical and Bill Leahy certainly did make a magnificent speech to them.

Finally, in the Supreme Court the American Medical Asso-

---

[1] See *United States* v. *American Medical Assn.*, 28 F. Supp. 752 (D. C. D. C. 1939), rev'd, 110 F. 2d 703 (C. A. D. C. 1940); 130 F. 2d 233 (C. A. D. C. 1942), aff'd, 317 U. S. 519 (1943).

[2] See *Federal Base Ball Club* v. *National League*, 259 U. S. 200 (1922).

ciation contended that it was a labor union and could, therefore, act like Mr. Petrillo. The Supreme Court rejected that contention. Since most of the doctors that I came in contact with were very bitter about the activities of labor unions it was very amusing to find them relying on the labor cases as a last resort.

I wish you luck in your argument with your Medical Association friend. However, I will give you 2-1 that no form of argument makes any impression on him whatever. It has been my experience that any group, whether from labor or industry or the profession, which gets itself in a position where it thinks it has special privileges will fight for them with complete intolerance and that John L. Lewis and Dr. Fishbein are brothers under the skin. This has been true, however, for 6,000 years so there is no point in being concerned about it.

With best regards,

Sincerely,
Thurman Arnold

August 5, 1949

Mr. Lingan A. Warren, President
Safeway Stores, Incorporated
P. O. Box 660
4th and Jackson Streets
Oakland 4, California

Dear Mr. Warren:

Business Week has referred to me your two letters of July 21, 1949, and has asked me for a comment.

You state that Safeway has a moral right to get goods at a lower price than its competitors if the law permits it and if by virtue of its buying power it is able to obtain that advantage.

I suppose this is true and that no businessman is immoral who follows the statutes and decisions of the courts with respect to his business conduct. However, as is apparent from my interview I was not discoursing on morals but discussing the economic questions of absentee ownership. I am convinced that absentee control of industries which can be effectively conducted by local concerns is an economic evil. I further think that prior to the depression it had grown on such a large scale as to be one of the principal causes of the lack of purchasing power of outlying areas.

I therefore argued in my interview with Business Week that large nationwide operations from an economic point of view should be confined to the single services which could not be carried on efficiently by local concerns. I used Coca-Cola as an example of a concern that had made tremendous profits by following this policy—by being the servant of local industry instead of its master. A contrary policy I believe leads to draining local communities dry of their capital and their income. Where it is legal it seems to me against the economic philosophy of the antitrust laws and the structure of business which finally results, one which I believe inevitably leads to actual violation of the antitrust laws. . . .

* * * *

Cordially yours,
Thurman Arnold

March 6, 1951

Dear . . . :

At our conference in . . . you indicated your interest in tax legislation which would permit a corporation to divest itself of subsidiaries without tax liability where the purpose was decentralization and more efficient management.

There has been considerable activity in Congress in this direction recently and it may be that there is a chance of passing such legislation in connection with the next Revenue Bill. The Treasury has always opposed and will probably continue to oppose. It has insisted that the tax bill be an insurance policy against any possible tax avoidance regardless of conflicts with antitrust policy. It may be that one of the reasons why efforts to get this relief have failed in the past is that the only analysis of the problem has been by tax lawyers who have not sufficiently emphasized the conflict with antitrust policy.

Your idea represents a much needed change in our tax law. The revenue provisions with respect to divestiture or decentralization of large business have been in direct conflict with our traditional antitrust policy. Voluntary decentralization of corporate enterprises which have become too large is preferable to government decrees provided it is done sincerely by men who believe in competition. Yet a tax penalty is put on any businessman who attempts to exercise his business judgment for purposes which promote decentralization. Certainly the voluntary action of businessmen who believe in decentralization should not be thus discouraged. It is in accord with the original purpose of the Sherman Act which contemplated private enforcement. The original intent of Congress was that the government would play only a small part in antitrust enforcement. The treble damage provision was passed to permit men engaged in industry to police themselves.

In addition, . . . , it has now become difficult for a parent with a large number of subsidiaries to conduct its operations without danger of antitrust liability. That doctrine is that a parent and a wholly-owned subsidiary are not to be treated as a single trader. Agreements between them or a joint policy arrived at by oral consultation may be prosecuted as a conspiracy. Unless the parent and subsidiary actually compete in prices and over the same territory there is a possible liability which might be difficult for a large concern to avoid. Yet if the parent seeks to avoid that liability by divesting itself of its subsidiary, it is penalized under the tax law.

When the Public Utility Holding Company Act of 1935 was passed, an attempt to restore competition in public utilities, a similar problem was presented to Congress. It was solved by making the dissolution of holding companies free from tax. Similar relief is urgently needed for companies in other fields which voluntarily decentralize. These arguments have never been satisfactorily answered by the Treasury. Its objection to your idea relates solely to possible tax dodging. Throughout the history of the attempts to bring tax law in accordance with the policy of the Sherman Act the Treasury has opposed proposals like yours on this ground.

It does not seem to me to be difficult to distinguish the transfer of corporate assets to a subsidiary for the purpose of tax dodging and the splitting off of a portion of the company's business for the purpose of efficiency of management and decentralization. The one is a rational move with business objectives. Liquidation of part of the business is not contemplated.

* * * *

The standards of a legitimate business purpose as opposed to tax evasion are fairly simple in nature and could be readily met in most bona fide split-off proposals. However, the psychology of the Bureau of Internal Revenue is such that there might be some resistance to such split-offs and the Bureau of Internal Revenue might be very sparing in the exercise of its power to grant the necessary approval, despite clear expressions of congressional purpose.

Accordingly, it might perhaps be considered desirable to adopt a different standard and permit another agency of the government to make the initial determination. Thus, if a standard were established in terms of (a) decreasing concentration of economic power, or (b) limiting the size of industrial enterprise by permitting disposal of properties which can be more efficiently managed independently, or (c) increasing the number of independently operated business enterprises, the nature of standards would make it appropriate to grant jurisdiction to the Department of Justice or the Federal Trade Commission to make the necessary findings and grant the tax relief. This is particularly appropriate in the light of the newly granted authority of these agencies over sales of assets under the newly passed Celler Bill. Once such a finding has been made, the Bureau of Internal Revenue would find it difficult to quarrel with the finding or to deny a tax exemption.

* * * *

You may be skeptical about giving the Department of Justice such power. It is obvious that either the Department or the Federal Trade Commission could use their authority to approve a tax free divestiture as a lever to obtain compliance with respect to complaints or proceedings to enforce the antitrust laws. Thus, for example, an exemption might be refused unless larger spin-offs than were proposed by the parent corporation were made or else on condition that the company take undesirably restrictive action to assure the immediate independence of the business split-off. Since one of the principal purposes of your idea is to increase the voluntary responsibility of individual businessmen and to decrease the necessity of government interference, if approval were required from the Department, the use of its power thus granted as a lever would have to be carefully guarded against.

* * * *

If you have any suggestions, please let me know. My own notion is that if the Antitrust Division could be interested, it would be of great assistance. There is a prevailing idea that when a group of tax attorneys advocate a measure they are seeking some hidden advantage for their clients. This would be rebutted by a presentation of the problem by the Department of Justice, if they could be induced to do so.

Sincerely,
Thurman Arnold

November 10, 1952

Mr. James C. Derieux
Collier's National Weekly
426 Homer Building
601 Thirteenth Street, N. W.
Washington, D. C.

Dear Mr. Derieux:

You asked me to outline three articles on the general problems of the antitrust laws.[1] My present ideas, which may not work out exactly in this form, are as follows:

---

[1] See Arnold, "Depression—Not In Your Lifetime", *Collier's*, April 25, 1953, p. 24.

The first article.

An antitrust program to be effective must not be inconsistent with the probable business development of this country. I have, therefore, written some broad generalizations as to what I think our future economic course will be, and indicated how the fundamental principles of the antitrust laws fit into that picture. These ten pages will probably not appear as I have written them but they will give you an idea of my initial approach.

The balance of the first article will be a discussion of the character of big business today with which the antitrust laws must deal. It is my belief that there must be a new approach to the problem of size in any rational program of antitrust enforcement. . . .

The article will close with a brief description of antitrust procedure. The terms of the law are broad enough and the procedure sufficiently elastic so that it can fit in with a rational economic program devoted to business expansion of American corporations at home and abroad. The difficulties in the past have not been with their size but rather with the mercantilistic policy followed by many great corporations to engage in purely local business, and thus to prevent the development of local capital and purchasing power.

The second article.

The second article will be devoted to a discussion of the problem of size in business enterprise and the present belief held in some quarters that the object of the antitrust laws is to make little ones out of big ones. This is not my view. I shall use as an illustration The Coca-Cola Company. Coca-Cola does not own its bottlers. It thus builds up independent wealth in every state of the union and also abroad. It is the largest purchaser of sugar in the world. It does not own any sugar plantations or refineries. . . . It creates a market which did not exist before. It gives local industry a chance to serve that market at a cost which would be impossible without Coca-Cola's tremendous organization. It makes its independent suppliers rich. In a very real sense Coca-Cola is exporting capital in creating international economic ties. Recently in France Coca-Cola was banned partly on account of the efforts of the Communist party. The law was quickly repealed because Frenchmen were making money out of Coca-Cola. I would not attempt to lay down a pattern for other industries, but simply use Coca-Cola as an illustration of how size can be a method of creating wealth in outlying areas. Certainly a curb on the expansion of Coca-Cola . . . would be an uneconomic program.

The article will also deal briefly on how the transition from a Government-supported market to a market in which private industry exported the necessary capital can be made. In conclusion, I would outline an antitrust program consistent with what I believe are the probable developments toward a free market.

The third article.

The third article would deal with the problem of labor unions, now free to violate the antitrust laws. There are many programs to bring labor under the antitrust laws now being debated. The program most frequently urged by business is to prohibit nationwide collective bargaining by labor unions. I seriously doubt if that is a feasible program in the light of the national and international character of expanding big business. My own view is that labor unions cannot be cut into smaller units for bargaining purposes. If I am right, the question arises as to how the use of that tremendous power may be curbed. In general the Taft-Hartley Act is not bad. Its defect in my view is that it puts the routine power to curb labor unions in the National Labor Relations Board. This is like putting the enforcement of the antitrust laws against big business in a government department devoted to the interests of big business. Labor unions can and do crush small businesses with strikes which have no legitimate labor objective and small business has no effective remedy. The Labor Board is either too busy or unsympathetic. I would restore the private injunction in cases where strikes were not for some legitimate labor purpose. I would expect to define these purposes.

In connection with putting the power in the President of the United States to decide whether, in the case of a national emergency such as the steel strike, an injunction suit should be brought against labor, my view is that such power should not be in a purely political office. Whatever party is in power, the question of gaining or losing labor support is one that will be at the heart of every decision.

I have not had time to reflect on these views and I may modify some of them after consultation with others. All I can do now is give you a general idea of what I intend to talk about.

Sincerely,
Thurman Arnold

April 21, 1955

Mr. Eugene Lyons
Senior Editor
The Reader's Digest
Pleasantville, New York

Dear Mr. Lyons:

You have asked me for a criticism of the article on labor. It is, of course, well written but is so confused in its objectives and its analyses that I think it will do a great deal more harm than good to the cause which we both support, i.e., bringing labor within the antitrust laws in a limited way.

The bias of the article is apparent in the first paragraph where the author says that for half a century there has been a tireless crusade to protect the public by enforcing the Sherman Act. And on page 3—for half a century thereafter the Government had moved against all monopolies in restraint of trade, whether set up by business men or labor leaders. This is complete nonsense. Labor has a very just cause for complaint because of antitrust prosecution since the *Danbury Hatters'* case.[1] The fact that the antitrust laws were effectively used to break up unions while at the same time business combines were not prosecuted at all is clear from even a casual reading of the cases prior to the Norris-LaGuardia Act. I recall in 1929 when I was Dean at West Virginia thousands of injunctions were issued by the judge against people who were literally starving.

But from reading the article one would think that all this time labor was being treated under the Sherman Act on the

---
[1] See *Loewe* v. *Lawlor*, 208 U.S. 274 (1908).

same basis as industry. An informed reader would, therefore, drop the article the minute he read the first two pages.

Furthermore, looking at the article as a whole, it gives the impression that one of our chief economic problems is the inefficiency of labor. This is simply not so. Our national production, which was $244,000,000,000 at the peak of the war, when every resource was strained, is now close to $400,000,000,000 and is zooming out of sight. Automation in factories is proceeding so that today an hour's work by an American laborer is worth twice as much as any other labor in the world. In the vast areas of mass production industries the increase of wages have provided markets for the products which would not otherwise exist.

Against this background your author attacks "labor monopolies". He cites a large number of instances of labor conspiracies in restraint of trade which are a far different thing. Interspersed with them is the Brooklyn Eagle strike which would seem to indicate that he thinks the right to strike should be in some way curbed if the objective is not economic. He appears to be attacking the power of a large union to make an unreasonable decision to ask for higher wages. While the Brooklyn Eagle strike was unfortunate nevertheless it's hard to imagine the court deciding that the union could not strike because the employer could not afford it, and deciding this difficult economic problem as a basis in a prosecution for violation of the Sherman Act. Such questions are completely ignored by your author. He cites unreasonable restraints of trade from 1938 on. He combines them with strikes for higher wages. He makes a completely unanalytical attack on the Taft-Hartley Act and comes out with the visionary idea that if our Federal courts were to be given all these questions to decide we would in some way be better off.

He attacks the union shop on logical but completely visionary grounds. It is in effect an article attacking the power of the nationwide union because of a number of abuses found in a limited area of the economy, transportation, printing and the building trades. He bolsters it up by saying that the Government's protection of the public against business restraints of trade has been constant and unremitting at a time when the Attorney General of the United States has issued a report recommending that the antitrust laws be weakened in their application against business.

It is this position which has constantly defeated in the committees before which I have testified any rational solution of restraints of trade in building, transportation and a few other fields.

The fact is that in the areas of our economy which have been able to assimilate mass production strong unions have contributed enormously to the assimilation of that production by raising the purchasing power of labor. In these industries the growing automation of plants is going to create more leisure for everyone. Strong unions are necessary in that process of adjustment. If the union shop is unconstitutional so is the movement for integrated bar associations spreading over the country where every lawyer must be compelled to pay dues. Perhaps your writer does not like the union shop. Nevertheless, his ideas about suddenly abolishing it are as visionary as those of any extremist.

If the problem represented by the examples that the author gives is put in its proper perspective, and if limited application of the antitrust laws to restraints of production is worked out there is a chance of doing some good. But an article which calls conspiracies in restraint of trade monopolies, which jumps from that to attacking the monopoly power of labor to strike for wages which the employer cannot afford, which goes on to attack welfare funds and fringe benefits which are going to be increasingly available to labor as production increases, which denounces the Taft Hartley Act in its entirety without analyzing the points in which it is weak, and which winds up with a broad generalization about enforcing the antitrust laws against labor which is meaningless because it is so broad, takes such an extreme position that its total effect is only to arouse the emotions of those who dislike labor unions. If you are going to win anybody over to curbing restraints of trade by labor in a few areas which mass production has not yet affected, it cannot be done by this unanalytical approach.

I am returning herewith the manuscript.

With best regards,

Sincerely,
Thurman Arnold

February 27, 1958

Mr. Arthur Krock
1701 K Street, N. W.
Washington 6, D. C.

Dear Arthur:

Thank you for your letter. My comment on George Lodge's letter is as follows:

Labor unions are the only organizations which are exempt

from the antitrust laws. Even railroads are liable in spite of the Interstate Commerce Commission. Farm cooperatives are liable in spite of their power to control the supply and fix prices. Labor is the only type of organization which has achieved complete exemption.

Of course, like farm cooperatives labor must be exempt to the extent of fixing the price of labor if it can by collective action. But where the concerted action of labor unions goes beyond collective bargaining for wages, hours, better conditions of work, etc., there is absolutely no excuse for not making them fully liable under the Sherman Act.

The exemption of labor has actually worked to the detriment of unions like Walter Reuther's and to the enhancement of power of unions like the Teamsters. The Teamsters union is the fastest growing union in the United States. They get their power by their control of transportation. They can hot-cargo any employer. They use this power of hot cargo to expand their organizational power.

Under the Taft-Hartley Act, to refuse to deliver goods to any business concern with whom the Teamsters do not have a direct relationship of employer and employee is an unfair labor practice. But in actual operation this is meaningless. The only way of enforcing the unfair labor practice is through the National Labor Relations Board. That Board has been so sympathetically inclined to labor that the cases where it will ask for an injunction are very rare indeed. Hence the Teamsters are able to use the secondary boycott with impunity.

But even if we had a labor board willing and anxious to stamp out the abuse of the secondary boycott, they couldn't possibly police the entire United States. Congress would never appropriate that amount of money. The best and most continuous type of enforcement of the antitrust laws is, of course, the private suit for injunction or damages. As the law is at present, the private individual can find himself cut off from supplies by the Teamsters and he can do nothing about it.

It is true, of course, that the Act does allow a suit for damages but he would be out of business before such a suit pursued its weary way through the trial and appellate courts. So, there are practically no suits for damages against unions for secondary boycott.

The Supreme Court of the United States has added to the difficulties by holding that when the Taft-Hartley Act was passed it vested in the Labor Relations Board complete jurisdiction over all illegal practices of unions. The case of *Gus* v. *Utah*[1] shows the extreme to which that doctrine has gone. In that case a small manufacturer with a business of about $100,000 a year was the victim of an illegal secondary boycott. He appealed to the National Labor Relations Board. The National Labor Relations Board answered that they would not intervene and ask for an injunction because the interstate commerce involved was not sufficient, although there was some. Whereupon, the employer sought and obtained an injunction from the Labor Board of the State of Utah. The Supreme Court reversed on the ground that the entire jurisdiction was in the Labor Board and the State of Utah was excluded from giving the employer relief. It was pointed out to the Court that the employer was in a bad situation. His business was being destroyed by an illegal act and all rights to protect it were taken

---

[1] See *Gus* v. *Utah Labor Relations Board*, 353 U. S. 1 (1957).

away. The Supreme Court said in effect that that was too bad, it was the intent of Congress to strip him of his property by denying him legal protection.

How your friend George Lodge can defend this practice I do not know. His letter is a bunch of generalities. He wants to regulate instead of leaving the matter to the courts where it belongs. It is a typical example of the regulation-minded government official and these people are just as wrong-headed whether they are in the New Deal or in the Eisenhower Administration.

We recently took a case up to the Supreme Court of the United States from Tennessee. There, two businesses were involved and they were in the same building. The employees in one business struck. The Teamsters threw up a picket line which of course was a secondary boycott and illegal, thereby depriving both concerns of supplies.

Both manufacturers sought an injunction against the common carrier, a trucking company, under state law for not delivering goods. The common carrier answered that it couldn't deliver goods because of their employees' refusal. Thereupon the court enjoined the Teamsters Union from interfering with its order against the common carrier. Some of the Teamsters were fined for interference with the court order. This was affirmed by the Supreme Court of Tennessee. The Supreme Court of the United States granted certiorari and reversed the Supreme Court of Tennessee.[1]

Curiously enough, these secondary boycotts do nobody any good except the Teamsters. Reuther couldn't effectively use a secondary boycott.

---

[1] See *McCrary* v. *Aladdin Industries*, 355 U.S. 8 (1957).

The responsibility for the power of Hoffa and Beck is directly on people who think like your friend Lodge.

If you will look back in the *Reader's Digest* you will find two articles on how I think the antitrust laws should be applied to labor. I think they were in the year 1943.

With best regards, in which Frances joins,

Sincerely,
Thurman Arnold

STATEMENT BY THURMAN ARNOLD
Before House Committee on the District of Columbia
On H. R. 7375
(For Release July 29, 1959)

I appear before the Committee as the representative of a number of independent retail liquor dealers in the District who are opposed to H. R. 7375.

This bill would establish compulsory resale price maintenance for all alcoholic beverages sold in the District. . . .

* * * *

We understand that it is further argued that the bill would promote the health and welfare of the District by preventing poor people who cannot afford the increase in prices from becoming alcoholics. Obviously the alcoholic himself would not be curbed by higher prices because he must have his liquor whatever it costs. However, those who are on a low budget and have not yet become alcoholics could no longer afford to drink enough liquor to bring on this disease and thus they would be saved by the price system from a drunkard's grave. Thus, through the mechanics of price fixing, the privilege and/or danger of becoming an alcoholic would be limited to the well-to-do.

I entertain a serious doubt as to the validity of this reasoning. I am informed that obesity is more prevalent than alcoholism and a greater threat to the national health. But I have not yet heard the suggestion that this danger should be eliminated by raising the prices of high-caloried foods. To protect the national health by price fixing seems to me an extraordinarily oblique method of attacking the problem.

* * * *

The dealers whom I represent are small, independent merchants. They should be left free to exercise their independent business judgment with respect to prices they will charge. This policy encourages competition. It promotes efficiency. It gives the consumer a better deal. The giant distilleries and wholesalers should not be given the power of life and death over these independent merchants. They should not be allowed to reap huge profits at the expense of the consumers in the District. H. R. 7375 should be rejected.

VII

On Insanity and Obscenity and the Law

"The great advance which the opinion {in the Durham case} will make lies in the fact that a priest-like tribunal has formally recognized mental disease as the controlling factor in an insanity case rather than sin."

"Such laws {making obscenity a crime} are passed because most men are stimulated by erotica and at the same time they are ashamed of it."

March 29, 1955

Mr. Warren P. Hill
Professor of Law
Ohio State University
Columbus, Ohio

Dear Professor Hill:

I have been so busy that this is the first opportunity I have had to comment on your article.[1] I am, as you may suspect, immensely pleased with it. In fact, it is the best article I have ever read on the subject. If you think I am biased because you have made me the subject of the article I can inform you that everyone else in the office, including those who worked on the *Durham* case,[2] is most enthusiastic.

I have no quarrel with anything you say in the article. Our chief difference appears to be on the practical consequences of the new rule. For example, you seem to think, though I am not at all sure of this, that there are certain practical consequences involved apart from public respect and deference to our trial procedure as a symbol. For example, you state in footnote 40 that "the probable effect of the new rule will be to increase the number of criminal defendants who are admitted under indefinite stay to the already overcrowded mental hospitals of the District".

My experience as a jury lawyer convinces me that the new rule will have no effect whatever in this respect. I predicted that Durham would be as quickly convicted under the new rule

---

[1] See Hill, *The Psychological Realism of Thurman Arnold*, 22 U. of Chicago L. R. 377 (1955).
[2] *Durham* v. *U. S.*, 214 F. 2d 862 (C. A. D. C. 1954).

as he was under the old, which proved to be true. And I will give you any odds you ask that the Court of Appeals will not reverse the conviction in spite of the fact that the evidence as I view it shows an almost conclusive case. They would, I guess, have recourse to reasoning such as I used in the *Fisher* case. Durham, though unquestionably insane, is a menace to the community. Nothing could do more harm to the cause of those who advocate the new rule than to have him turned loose and commit some more crimes which he probably would do. It is unlikely that the Court of Appeals would put the rule to such a strain. (This of course is not the kind of an argument you advance in a law review article. It is, however, a practical consequence which means the new rule will turn loose more criminals than the old.)

Indeed, I suspect that the new rule will make it more difficult to acquit, at least in cases of some emotional crimes, than the old one . . . .

There was never any difficulty in getting psychiatrists under the old rule to testify for a fee. You suggest (top of page 385) that I seem to be saying that it might be socially disastrous to let the jury know that the criminal was not a breed apart. But under the old rule, as you will note from the *Holloway* and *Fisher* cases,[1] all of the symptoms of the accused were given to the jury.

[Judge] Bazelon owes the opportunity to write this decision to the attempt of Judge Holtzoff to make the old rule, which was very elastic indeed, into a hard and fast dogma to be strictly applied. Judge Bazelon took the offered opportunity and

---

[1] *Holloway* v. *U. S.*, 148 F. 2d 665 (C. A. D. C. 1945); *Fisher* v. *U. S.*, 149 F. 2d 28 (C. A. D. C. 1945).

his decision may well be a landmark in the gradual change of our attitude towards crime. It is claimed that the new rule will permit a better class of psychiatrists to appear in court than those now willing to testify about right and wrong. This I doubt. Under our trial system no attorney for the defense is going to pay a psychiatrist fees for testifying unless he is going to be pretty positive and doctrinaire. Neither will the prosecution hire him unless they are equally positive on the other side. It is the law of supply and demand which will exclude the more objective men.

Your article shows that you realize that the criminal trial is a symbolic battle in which the state is protecting its citizens from their enemies and at the same time being just to them. Men simply cannot be objective if they take part in any public contest on which they must choose sides. Psychiatrists are no exception. I argued with my psychiatric friends about the denazification proceeding in Germany which violated every concept of due process. It was as bad as the worst Congressional investigation. Their instinctive reaction was that I must be some kind of a Nazi.

So long as the issue to be tried is whether defendant is to be *blamed* for his conduct and tried in a society which will not pay for the care of delinquents we are not going to get much difference in results. The great advance which the opinion will make lies in the fact that a priest-like tribunal has formally recognized mental disease as the controlling factor in an insanity case rather than sin.

You indicate that perhaps judges would be better than juries. In my view they would be much worse. The fantastic difference in treatment of criminals between one judge and another with respect to sentences is shocking. Judges are much more under pressure than juries because juries have comparative anonymity. They are fearful of criticism. Indeed there are very few like Bazelon. He was extremely fortunate in having an opportunity given by the trial court who tried to narrow the former loose and easy application of the right and wrong test. By making it too tough he made it impractical.

He was also fortunate in having two colleagues willing to embark on a course that might be criticized as judicial legislation. I was surprised at the lack of criticism although the Washington Star did go after him pretty hard. But in general the decision was accepted as sensible.

The practical effect of Bazelon's decision is to provide the escape which used to be provided by the phrase "irresistible impulse". This was offensive both to those who wanted the criminal trial to represent the punishment of sin and those who wanted to apply the point of view of psychiatry. Psychiatrists cannot talk in such terms. They have the further disadvantage of making possible purely inflammatory appeals. The complicated words of psychiatry give a calmer and more rational appearance to a trial.

You may well ask since I am so enthusiastic about Bazelon's opinion why I did not write one to the same effect. The reason was, as you make clear from your article, that I thought that the right or wrong test was more necessary to a public sense of justice than it appears to be now.

My opinion[1] at least had the advantage of arousing the psychiatrists. They liked parts of it, they hated the conclu-

---
[1] See *Holloway* v. *United States*, 148 F. 2d 665 (C.A. D.C. 1945).

sion. I have appeared at least six times before groups of psychiatrists and once before the national convention in Atlantic City to explain my opinion. The more they talked the more determined they were to obtain a more dignified place in criminal procedure than was possible under my analysis. I, therefore, should be credited with an assist to Bazelon and am flattered that he used parts of the opinion which were acceptable to psychiatry as a stepping-stone to his radical and, I think, proper change.

The problem will never be solved until the sentencing power now exercised by federal judges with a shocking inconsistency is transferred to a competent board not operating under the glare of publicity. That time is a long way off but it will come sooner because of the opinion in the *Durham* case.

Sincerely,
Thurman Arnold

{The following are extracts from Thurman Arnold's Brief for Respondent-Appellant in Vermont v. Verham News Corporation in the Supreme Court of Vermont. The brief was filed in 1959 on behalf of Playboy magazine. Following the filing of this brief, the State dismissed the criminal information against the defendant.}

* * * *

But an obscenity statute rests on a different basis. It is in its essence a moral declaration on the part of the legislature, a recognition of a taboo which is as old as history. Such laws are passed because most men are stimulated by erotica and at the same time they are ashamed of it. Society requires a public denunciation of this almost universal sin whether or not it leads to positive harmful conduct.

Thus from time immemorial laws making obscenity a crime have been a psychological requirement of a society which wants to be considered moral and virtuous.[5] Even in ancient Greece, a society not distinguished for its puritanism, Plato in 378 B.C. urged that the *Odyssey* be expurgated for children's reading. In ancient Rome Ovid's book "The Art of Love",—a book which today freely circulates because it is a classic, caused the emperor Augustus to banish Ovid in 7 A.D. The fact that laws against obscenity do not have a rational or scientific basis, but rather symbolize a moral taboo, does not make them any the less necessary. They are important because men feel that without them the state would be lacking in moral standards.

But because obscenity statutes represent a moral taboo and not a rational process the field of pornography is full of curious contradictions. For example, distinguished artists are not prone to committing or assisting in the commission of ordinary crime. But the literature of obscenity contains some of our greatest names. Mark Twain, whose dialogue called "1601" is today widely but secretly circulated, wrote to a Cleveland librarian, "If there is a decent word findable in it it is because I overlooked it."[6] Great painters have lent their talents to producing erotic material so extreme that it had to be secretly circulated. Such names include Hogarth, Rowlandson, Aubrey Beardsley, Rubens, Rembrandt, Jan Steen, Michelangelo, Raphael, Tintoretto, Titian, Boucher and Rodin. In music Gilbert and Sullivan produced an obscene musical play called "The Sod's

---

[5] The historical discussion which follows is drawn from Ginzburg, *An Unhurried View of Erotica* (1958). [All footnotes in the selections from this brief are in the original.]

[6] Id. at 77.

Opera". Yet Sullivan was the man who wrote "Onward Christian Soldiers". The list could be extended indefinitely. One of the most widely read pornographic articles was written by Benjamin Franklin; another star in this galaxy was Eugene Field.

There is a certain high comedy in the contradictions which roam throughout the area of pornography. At the same time that men insist on suppressing obscene literature and punishing those who write it they enthusiastically go on collecting it and preserving it in libraries of priceless value. The Catholic Church is a leader in the fight against obscenity. Yet it maintains in the Vatican library the most famous collection of erotica in the world, consisting of 25,000 volumes and 100,000 prints.[7] Ralph Ginzburg in his recent book states that among libraries the Vatican erotica "is probably most accessible to the non-professional bibliophile".[8] Erotic material was collected by that good churchman J. P. Morgan. Henry E. Huntington, the railway magnate, had the greatest collection in the West. Yale, Princeton and Harvard have collections of erotica.[9]

Access to this material is ordinarily made difficult. But this is not true of the Library of Congress which has the largest collection of erotica in the United States. Anyone over sixteen may see the books. In addition, the Union catalogue of the Library of Congress publicly lists existing erotica works giving information which could be used by any pornographic bookseller. Logically it might seem that the Library was contributing to the crime of obscenity but no sensible man would want

---

[7] Id. at 103.
[8] Id. at 107.
[9] Id. at 103-105.

to change its present practices. Thus the moral problem of obscenity is as full of inconsistencies and contradictions as was another moral crusade, i.e., the enforcement of prohibition where good citizens wanted liquor and prohibition at the same time.

* * * *

Assuming that a line has to be drawn between material so offensively obscene that it is a crime to distribute it and material which is merely suggestive of sex, the question before this Court is where and how to draw that line. Two considerations should, we think, be in the mind of the Court. First, the line should not be drawn in such a way as to interfere with the literary artist. Moral censorship as it has existed, for example, in Boston, which went so far as to condemn H. L. Mencken's *Mercury* Magazine while at the same time burlesque shows were running full blast at the old Howard Theatre, is indefensible. Yet such is the zeal of reformers that the banning of works of real merit is an inevitable consequence unless the definition of obscenity is strictly limited. Over the ages it has been proved that it is impossible for moral reformers to let good books alone. It is the responsibility of the courts to prevent zealots from curbing art in trying to cut down on the number of impure thoughts per capita among the general public.

Heretofore the most frequently applied test of obscenity was whether the material in question had a tendency to produce lustful thoughts. This test is tempered by giving allowance to the serious character of artistic merit of the work as a whole. This test has proved useless in the past. It puts courts in the role of literary critics, a task for which they are unfitted. It achieves fantastically inconsistent results.

Another evil of the commonly applied "lustful thoughts" test in judging obscenity is its tendency to create attitudes towards sex which are akin to fetishism. For example, in 1900, when women were required to bathe fully clothed and bare legs were a mark of indecency, youths were stimulated by the sight of an ankle or a calf. Certainly no one can call this a healthy reaction. In 1911, a book was widely sold named "Three Weeks" in which the obscene passages consisted only of pages of asterisks at appropriate places. The book was passed from hand to hand in every college. Certainly it is unhealthy to be stimulated by asterisks. Human beings can be trained like Pavlov's dog so that they are stimulated by sights and sounds completely unrelated to the things they desire. A strict standard of obscenity contributes to such unhealthy training.

Furthermore, the broader the definition of what is forbidden, the greater number of objects become obscene but stimulating fetishes—solely because they have been forbidden. The more tolerant standards of today as compared with those of 1900 have reduced the number of indecent works to a minimum and thus have reduced the amount of "obscenity" in our culture. Certainly we have today a healthier attitude toward sex in literature or art than the days when fig leaves had to be put on statues. Taking the pin-up girls away from American soldiers would not make their minds more pure. It would only mean that they would be aroused by some less healthy or attractive substitute.

The moral censor who tries to make all literature decent is like a man who wants everything up and nothing down. He may succeed in getting things higher and higher but some of them will always be down or else none of them will be up. For example, at the turn of the century the old Police Gazette had a nation-wide pornographic appeal. A dance called the Can-Can in which the chorus girls kicked up legs covered with black stockings was wicked and highly stimulating. Today a person with an appetite for pornography would not pay ten cents to see either the magazine or the dance. This is how censorship makes material sexually stimulating which would not have any stimulation at all if that censorship did not exist. And that is why anything but the most tolerant standards creates an unhealthy psychology.

* * * *

If we are right in these observations a court in applying an obscenity statute should construe it to include only the most extreme forms of erotic material. If this attitude is not taken the result of the broad censorship will be to create an artificial erotic appeal in writing which without it would be considered as harmless.

Certainly the magazines before the Court in this case are harmless from any healthy standards. They contain pictures of very pretty and undraped women. They contain smoking room stories. But men have enjoyed this kind of material from the beginning of time. To condemn these magazines is to turn the clock back to the 19th Century when men could be stimulated by the sight of a woman's ankle. . . .

* * * *

INDEX OF NAMES

Aarvold, (Judge) C.D. 31
Adams Sherman 38
Arnold, Mrs. C. P. 4, 35
Arnold, George 4, 7
Arnold, Mrs. Thurman 3, 5, 12, 15, 22, 23, 24, 32, 35, 36, 52, 127
Arnold, Thurman, Jr. 4, 7
Aylsworth, L. E. 109
Bailey, Dorothy 18, 69, 70, 71, 72, 90, 98
Bazelon, (Judge) David 132, 134, 135
Beck, David 127
Berle, Adolph A., Jr. 94
Black, (Justice) Hugo 15, 43
Boikan, Sergius M. 52
Bogle, Lawrence 73
Bujalski, Ann S. 28
Burton, (Justice) Harold H. 16
Calhoun, Philo C. 15
Cardozo, (Justice) Benjamin 56
Cella, Louis B. 41
Chafee, Zechariah, Jr. 84
Chamberlain, John 107
Christ, Carl 53
Clark, (Judge) Charles E. 11, 12, 23, 90
Clark, Mrs. Charles E. 11, 22
Clifford, William 101
Condon, Edward A. 98
Cook, Alistair 102
Corwin, Edward S. 63
Dabney, Lewis M., Jr. 22
Davies, John Peyton 98
Davies (Ambassador) Joseph E. 96

Derieux, James C. 116
Dewey, John 56
Dixon, George 27
Donaldson, Norman 30
Douglas, (Justice) William O. 23
Douglas, Mrs. William O. 23
Edgerton, (Judge) Henry W. 72
Fishbein, Morris 111
Fleeson, Doris 43
Fly, James Lawrence 77
Fortas, Abe 3, 59, 63, 68, 83, 92
Frank, (Judge) Jerome 51
Freeman, Milton V. 63, 92
Frost, Robert 37, 38, 39

Gardner, George K. 70
Gates, Cassius E. 73
Ginzburg, Benjamin 101, 102
Ginzburg, Ralph 136, 137
Glenn, John R. 58

Hamilton, Walton H. 18, 33, 45, 46
Hamm, John C. 6
Harris, Crampton 43
Henderson, Leon 41, 42
Hergesheimer, Joseph 5, 77
Hill, Warner P. 131
Hiss, Alger 101, 102
Hoffa, James 127
Holmes, (Justice) Oliver Wendell 56
Holtzoff, (Judge) Alexander 69, 132
Hoover, J. Edgar 35
Hutchins, Robert M. 74

Ickes, Harold 44

Jackson, Gardner 101
Jackson, (Justice) Robert H. 33, 42, 43, 44
Josephson, Matthew 105
Kadish, Sanford 28, 29, 30, 31
Keezer, Dexter M. 106
Kerr, Chester 29, 31
Kilgore, (Senator) Harley M. 83
Krock, Arthur 123

Ladejinsky, Wolfe 98
Lane, Chester T. 90
Lattimore, Owen 71, 75, 78, 82, 87, 88
Leahy, William 110
Levy, Herbert Monte 78, 81
Lewis, John L. 109, 111
Livingston, Joseph A. 20
Lodge, George 123, 126, 127
Lovett, Robert A. 65
Lyons, Eugene 120

MacArthur, (General) Douglas 73
McGrath, J. Howard 68
McKelway, Benjamin M. 24, 26, 85
McLean, Evalyn Walsh 33, 35, 36
Martin, Edward M. 13
Mencken, H. L. 138
Miller, John S. 19
Murphy, (Justice) Frank 35, 36, 44

O'Mahoney, (Senator) Joseph C. 79, 82, 83
Oman, William M. 42

Oppenheimer, J. Robert 89, 98
Overholser, (Dr.) Winfred 38, 40

Padway, Joseph 24
Patterson, Cissie 35
Pegler, Westbrook 37
Peters, (Dr.) John P. 89, 90, 91 98, 99, 100
Petrillo, James 111
Pickett, Charles 52
Porter, Paul 3, 18, 68, 83, 92
Pound, Ezra 33, 37, 38, 39, 40
Pound, Mrs. Ezra 39, 40

Ranke, Mrs. Elisabeth Schmidt 3
Raymond, Fred 107
Reuther, Walter 124, 126
Ritner, Peter V. 84
Roosevelt, (President) Franklin D. 33, 40, 41, 51

Schlesinger, Arthur 51
Service, John Stewart 98
Seymour, Charles 90
Sturges, Wesley A. 12
Sullivan, Harry 58

Taft, (Senator) Robert A. 52
Titus, James E. 54
Todd, Hiram C. 88
Truman, (President) Harry S. 24

Waldrop, Frank C., 35, 51
Warren, Lingan A. 111
Wert, Thomas C. 57

Young, Owen D. 106
Youngdahl, (Judge) Luther W. 86, 87

CPSIA information can be obtained at www.ICGtesting.com
Printed in the USA
LVOW121223020513

331776LV00003B/321/P

9 781258 142650